Best Recipes from the

Farmer's Wife
COOKBOOK

Brimming with creative inspiration, how-to projects, and useful information to enrich your everyday life, Quarto Knows is a favorite destination for those pursuing their interests and passions. Visit our site and dig deeper with our books into your area of interest: Quarto Creates, Quarto Cooks, Quarto Homes, Quarto Lives, Quarto Drives, Quarto Explores, Quarto Gifts, or Quarto Kids.

© 2022 Quarto Publishing Group USA Inc.
Text © 2010, 2022 Quarto Publishing Group USA Inc.

Second edition published in 2022
First Published in 2010 by Voyageur Press, an imprint of The Quarto Group,
100 Cummings Center, Suite 265-D, Beverly, MA 01915, USA.
T (978) 282-9590 F (978) 283-2742 QuartoKnows.com

Voyageur Press titles are also available at discount for retail, wholesale, promotional, and bulk purchase. For details, contact the Special Sales Manager by email at specialsales@quarto.com or by mail at The Quarto Group, Attn: Special Sales Manager, 100 Cummings Center, Suite 265-D, Beverly, MA 01915, USA.

26 25 24 23 22   1 2 3 4 5

ISBN: 978-0-7603-6939-5

Digital edition published in 2022
eISBN: 978-0-7603-6940-1

Library of Congress Cataloging-in-Publication Data available

Design and page layout: Tango Media Publishing Services, LLC
Cover Image: Barv_Art/Shutterstock
Back Cover Photos, left to right: iStock.com/Lauri Patterson; Brent Hofacker/Shutterstock; Agave Studio/Shutterstock; tolin168/Shutterstock
See page 230 for photo and illustration credits.

Printed in China

Best Recipes from the

Farmer's Wife
COOKBOOK

Over 250 Blue-Ribbon Recipes

EDITED BY BEVERLY HUDSON

VOYAGEUR
PRESS

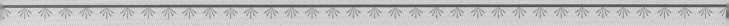

Contents

Introduction

❖

The Farmer's Wife, a monthly magazine published in Minnesota between the years 1893 and 1939, offered rural women both practical advice and a glimpse of the larger world around them. In an era long before the Internet and high-speed travel connected us all, the magazine aimed to offer community among hard-working rural women in many parts of the country, to provide a forum for their questions and concerns, and to assist them in the day-to-day goings-on about the farm. Topics covered in the magazine included raising chickens, slaughtering hogs, managing scant funds and dressing the children, keeping house, and running the kitchen.

The kitchen is where the farmer's wife really shone. She could be creative in the kitchen, letting her imagination run wild over stews, roasts, salads, casseroles, preserves, cakes, and cookies of her own invention. She could show off her skill, whipping up a simple, delicious meal and dessert of the utmost perfection. She could exercise one of the most esteemed qualities among country women—that of thrift, using the eggs, milk, butter, preserves, and other stores abundant on any farm—while at the same time showing love and care for her family through the hearty meals and delectable treats she offered them each and every day.

Issues of the magazine portray the farmer's wife as a woman willing and able to economize her time in the kitchen; a woman bent on nourishing her family, both body and soul; and a woman who understood the importance of laying up stores for the future.

The farmer's wife tackled the responsibility of feeding both family and neighbors with great seriousness and strict planning, preparing filling dishes for supper as well as tasty cakes and cookies for visitors. The farm woman prepared sweet but modest offerings to gladden the hearts of hard-working family members and friends.

This indispensable volume is a collection of our favorite recipes, culled from the *Farmer's Wife* magazines. The recipes in this book have been reprinted much as they appeared on the pages of the magazine, but with slight updates for readability and ease of use for contemporary cooks. Most recipes have been taken from issues spanning 1911–1939, and many were written by the magazine's own readers. In their language and ingredients, they reflect the style and manners of their times. Anyone accustomed to reading cookbooks will nevertheless feel right at home among the pages of this book. After all, the farmer's wife was nothing if not commonsensical, and so were her recipes.

Tips for Using This Book

Though we have taken some steps to update the recipes herein for contemporary cooks, anyone new to cookbooks—and, more particularly, historical cookbooks—is advised to follow the golden rule of the recipe: read it thoroughly, start to finish, and preferably more than once, before embarking. Make sure you understand the instructions and the order in which they must be carried out; check that you have all the ingredients at hand and assembled; and be sure to preheat your oven a good 20 to 30 minutes before you are ready to bake. Wherever possible, we have attempted to abolish confusing, misleading, or laborious instructions. There are some guidelines to remember, however, when using this cookbook.

Farm-Fresh Ingredients

First, the term *seasonings* would generally have been understood by the farmer's wife to mean salt and pepper. Efforts have been made in this book to differentiate between salt and pepper seasoning and the secondary meaning of the word, which includes other herbs, spices, and flavorings—these are listed separately on ingredients lists.

Farm women once had an ample supply of bacon and other drippings readily at hand, kept in a coffee can and used almost daily. Most contemporary cooks don't keep their drippings, so oil or butter can be substituted as appropriate. When a recipe calls for both bacon and drippings, the fat leftover from frying the bacon can, of course, be used for just this purpose.

In any recipe, shortening can be substituted for lard; "fat" can be interpreted as "butter"—use accordingly.

Aside from cottage cheese, which could be readily produced by pouring hot water over thick, sour milk (a common farm product), the farmer's wife did not make much cheese, unless she was engaged in its commercial manufacture. She had ample access to

"store" cheese, though, which is how she commonly referred to Cheddar. Recipes in the *Farmer's Wife* magazine sometimes referred specifically to other types of cheese, such as American or Parmesan; mostly, though, the original recipes are vague in the type of cheese to use. Experienced or adventurous cooks are encouraged to follow their instincts as to what sort of cheese might be used in any dish, but Cheddar is often a safe choice.

Honey was not necessarily a common farm staple—the farmer's wife more frequently used sugar in her cooking and baking. Recipes in the magazine almost always refer to "strained" honey, which is the clear, liquid version most of us buy these days, honey removed from the comb and strained free of wax and crystals. Any store-bought honey not in the comb will suffice for the recipes here.

Quite a number of the original *Farmer's Wife* baking recipes call for *sour milk*. According to Sandra Oliver, editor of *Food History News*, sour milk was a naturally occurring product on farms in the days before pasteurization, and it was very useful for baking. "The acidity in the sour milk interacted with the alkaline in the baking soda to make the gas that raised baked goods," she explains. We've substituted buttermilk in the recipes that call for sour milk. If you'd like to make your own sour milk, add 1 tablespoon of vinegar to 1 cup of "sweet" milk (a term the *Farmer's Wife* used to differentiate it from "sour" milk).

Measurements

1 pint = 2 cups
1 quart = 4 cups
1 peck = 8 quarts

Always sift flour once before measuring, and unless otherwise specified, use large eggs when eggs are called for in a recipe. Also, 1 square of Baker's chocolate refers to the 1-ounce variety, and rolled oats should be of the old-fashioned type, not the quick-cooking. The following are some other measurements you might need:

1 pound yields:

4 cups sifted all-purpose flour
4½ cups sifted cake flour
3½ cups graham flour
3 cups cornmeal
5½ cups rolled oats
2¼ cups white sugar
2½ cups brown sugar
2¾ cups powdered sugar
1⅓ cups molasses or honey
2 cups milk
4 cups nut meats, chopped
3 cups dried fruit

Some recipes in this book do not stipulate baking times. The following guidelines can be used:

For cookies: bake until just golden.

For cakes and breads: bake until the cake begins to pull away from the sides of the pan and a toothpick inserted in the center comes out clean. Also, for breads, tap the pan and listen for a hollow sound.

For custards: bake until just set.

For single-crust, filled pies: start in a hot oven (425°F to 450°F) for the first 10 minutes to crisp up the crust, then lower the temperature to 350°F to finish.

For unfilled pie shells: bake at 425°F for 18 to 20 minutes, or until lightly brown.

For unfilled tart shells: bake at 425°F for 12 minutes.

More than anything, this book wants to be used, not merely perused and admired. So please use it! And know that as you do, you are cooking up a bit of farmland history.

The 🍲 icon indicates the recipe requires a slow cooker for preparation.

Salads, Sandwiches, and Picnic Fare

Boston Baked Beans

February 1935

Though the humble bean may not be the star of any summer cookout, no one's plate should go without a serving or two of this smoky and tangy classic. In fact, slow-simmered, molasses-sweetened morsels are the reason Boston earned the nickname Beantown. Delicious straight out of the pot, they also taste great cooled down. Try serving leftover beans over scrambled eggs and toast for a protein- and fiber-rich breakfast.

MAKES ABOUT 12 CUPS

---

1 quart dried navy, pinto, or small white beans
½ to 1 tablespoon salt
½ tablespoon prepared mustard
1 cup hot water
1 small onion, chopped
¼ pound salt pork or bacon
3 tablespoons molasses

Rinse the beans, then put them in a container with a lid. Add enough cold water to cover the beans, put the lid on the container, and soak the beans overnight. In the morning, drain the beans, put them in a stock pot, cover them with fresh water, and cook them on low heat until their skins break, 45 to 50 minutes. Drain.

Preheat the oven to 250°F.

In a small bowl, mix the salt, mustard, and hot water together. Set aside.

Place the chopped onion in the bottom of an earthenware bean pot; pour in the beans. Score the rind of the salt pork (or chop the bacon). Bury the pork in the beans, leaving the rind exposed (or mix in the chopped bacon). Add the molasses and the seasonings mixture. Cover the bean pot and bake the beans for 6 to 8 hours. Add water as necessary to keep the beans from burning. Bake uncovered for the last hour.

Country Kitchen Salad

July 1936

SERVES 8

1 tablespoon vinegar

1 teaspoon salt

dash of pepper and cayenne

¼ teaspoon paprika

2 tablespoons oil

4 cups cold, cooked, cubed potatoes

1 or 2 cups chopped celery, cucumber, and/or sliced radishes

2 tablespoon chopped onion

4 hard-cooked eggs, cut into eighths

½ cup chopped sweet pickle

2 cups salad dressing

½ cup shredded lettuce

In a large bowl, combine the vinegar, salt, pepper, cayenne, paprika, and oil. Add the cubed potatoes and marinate them for about 1 hour.

Add the celery, cucumbers, radishes, onion, eggs, and sweet pickle. Pour in the dressing and toss to combine. As time allows, salad is improved by standing. Toss in lettuce just before serving.

With carrots: Add ½–¾ cup finely shredded carrots to the dressing, omitting some of the other vegetables.

Mayonnaise dressing: Replace some of the dressing with mayonnaise, if desired.

Marinating with sour cream: Omit the oil, and instead heat a ½ cup of sour cream with the vinegar and seasonings. Pour over the potatoes and let the mixture stand until cold before adding the other ingredients.

German Potato Salad

February 1928

SERVES 6

2 pounds potatoes

salt

¾ pound bacon

2 medium onions, sliced

½ cup vinegar

1 cup water

½ cup sugar

Boil the potatoes without peeling. Drain, cool, peel, and chop. Salt lightly.

Cut the bacon into pieces and fry, then drain on paper.

Add the onions to the bacon fat and cook them until they are translucent. Add the vinegar, water, and sugar to the onions. Stir to mix, bring to a boil, then add the potatoes. Serve the potato salad topped with the bacon.

Sloppy Joes on Toasted Buns

Utah Club Plate Luncheon, Submitted by Mrs. P. H. Rasmussen, October 1939

SERVES 12 TO 16

3 pounds lean ground beef
1 large yellow onion, chopped
1 cup chopped celery
⅓ cup olive oil
2 cups finely chopped green
    tomatoes, with all liquid
    reserved for the slow cooker
salt and pepper to taste
buns
butter

In a large skillet, brown the beef, onion, and celery in the olive oil over a medium-high heat. Transfer the cooked beef mixture to the slow cooker and add the green tomatoes and their juice. Salt and pepper to taste. Set the slow cooker to low and cook for 2 to 3 hours, until the meat is cooked through and the tomatoes have softened into a sauce. Check for seasoning.

Split the buns, toast them, spread butter on them, and top them with the beef mixture.

Chicken Salad

April 1929

SERVES 6

3 cups cold, leftover chicken, cubed
1½ cups chopped celery
1 teaspoon salt
2 hard-cooked eggs
½ to ¾ cup mayonnaise
crisp lettuce or sandwich bread

Combine the chicken, celery, and salt. Slice the eggs, saving 3 or 4 perfect slices for a garnish. Add the egg to the other ingredients and mix well with mayonnaise. Serve on crisp lettuce if available, or as a sandwich filling.

Egg Sandwich Filling

24 hard-cooked eggs
1 cup sifted breadcrumbs
1½ tablespoons lemon juice
2 teaspoons salt
salad dressing

Peel and chop the eggs. Add the breadcrumbs, lemon juice, and salt. Stir in enough salad dressing to make a paste.

Vegetable Sandwich Filling

March 1928

MAKES ABOUT 7 PINTS

1 cup sugar
4 tablespoons flour
1 teaspoon ground mustard
2 teaspoons salt
12 small red bell peppers
4 medium onions
1½ cups vinegar
½ cup water

In a small bowl, thoroughly mix together the sugar, flour, mustard, and salt. Set aside.

Finely mince the peppers and onions, then drain off the liquid. In a large bowl, mix all the ingredients together, then transfer the mixture to a pan and cook over medium heat for 20 minutes. Allow the filling to cool before spreading on bread or toast.

"Barbecued" Ribs

February 1939

SERVES 4

---

3 to 4 pounds spareribs, cut into
    individual pieces
2 tablespoons butter, melted
¼ cup vinegar
1 tablespoon Worcestershire sauce
1 tablespoon brown sugar
1 teaspoon celery salt (or regular
    salt, if you prefer)
1½ teaspoons mustard
2 tablespoons ketchup

In a large skillet, brown the spareribs on all sides over medium-high heat.

Meanwhile, mix together the butter, vinegar, Worcestershire sauce, brown sugar, celery salt, mustard, and ketchup in a bowl.

When the ribs are browned on all sides, transfer them to the slow cooker and spoon the sauce over them, turning to coat on all sides. Set the slow cooker to low and cook for 3 to 4 hours until the meat is very tender. Turn the ribs now and again to make sure all sides are immersed in the sauce to prevent them from drying out. Serve at once.

◆

Deviled Eggs

July 1914

SERVES 4

---

4 hard-cooked eggs
¼ teaspoon salt
½ teaspoon Dijon mustard
⅛ teaspoon pepper
1 teaspoon vinegar
2 teaspoon mayonnaise
paprika

Remove the shells from the eggs and cut each in half lengthwise.

Remove the yolks and put them in a medium-size bowl. Add the salt, Dijon mustard, pepper, vinegar, and mayonnaise and mash until smooth. Place a heaping spoonful of the yolk mixture into each egg half. Garnish with a sprinkle of paprika.

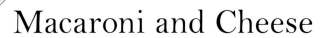

Macaroni and Cheese

October 1916

If you've never made macaroni and cheese from scratch, you won't believe how easy it is. In fact, you can make it in about the same amount of time that it takes to make a box of the yellow stuff. This velvety version goes beyond the saucepan by baking it with breadcrumbs for a bit of buttery crunch.

SERVES 4

1½ cups (½ pound) elbow macaroni
salt
1 cup thin White Sauce
    (see page 112)
½ cup grated cheese
1½ cups Buttered Crumbs
    (see page 116)

Preheat the oven to 350°F. Grease the bottom and sides of a 2-quart casserole dish.

Fill a large saucepan with water and bring it to a boil. Add salt in the proportion of 1 tablespoon for each quart. Add the macaroni and stir frequently to keep the macaroni from sticking to the bottom of the pan. Cook until it is just tender. (Different brands of macaroni cook at different rates; consult the instructions on the box.) Transfer the macaroni to a strainer, and set the strainer in a pan of cold water to remove the starch that causes the pieces to stick together.

Warm the white sauce, then add the grated cheese and mix until the cheese is melted and blended. Stir in the macaroni, then pour it into the prepared casserole dish and top with the buttered crumbs. Bake for 20 to 25 minutes, until brown and bubbly.

French Salad Dressing

April 1917

SERVES 4

2 tablespoons vinegar
6 tablespoons oil
½ teaspoon salt
¼ teaspoon pepper
paprika
fresh greens, for serving

Combine the vinegar, oil, salt, pepper, and paprika in a bowl. Beat steadily until thoroughly blended and thick. Serve on fresh greens.

Sweet Chocolate Sandwiches

September 1929

SERVES 2

2 ounces bittersweet chocolate
2 tablespoons unsweetened butter
1 cup powdered sugar
3 tablespoons heavy cream
⅔ cup finely chopped walnuts
butter
bread

Melt the chocolate in a double boiler. Add the butter, sugar, and cream and cook gently for 5 minutes. Add the nuts. Cool slightly and spread between buttered slices of bread.

Soups and Stews

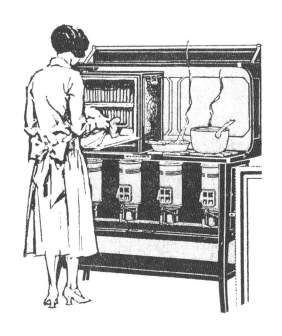

Chicken Rice Soup

1934

SERVES 8
---

2 medium onions, chopped
1½ teaspoons celery salt*
2 teaspoons salt*
¼ cup uncooked rice, rinsed
2 quarts (8 cups) chicken stock
½ cup minced uncooked chicken
1 teaspoon chopped parsley

In a large stock pot, add the onions, celery salt, salt, and rice to the stock. Cook for about 10 minutes, until the rice is half done. Add the minced chicken and cook for another 10 minutes. Garnish with the chopped parsley.

*Note: Adjust the amounts of salt and celery salt in accordance with the saltiness of your stock. If you are using store-bought broth, you will probably need less than is called for.

Egg Soup

July 1914

SERVES 6
---

3 pints (6 cups) beef stock
1 cup flour
1 egg
¼ teaspoon salt
¼ teaspoon baking powder

Heat the beef stock in a large saucepan.
Sift the flour into a medium-size bowl, then loosely stir in the egg, salt, and baking powder until all the flour is moistened. Stir the flour and egg mixture into the hot beef stock and cook for 5 minutes. Serve hot.

Potato Soup

May 1931

SERVES 4
---

2 cups diced peeled potatoes
1 slice from a large onion
1 cup boiling water
1 teaspoon salt
¼ teaspoon pepper
2 cups thin sour cream*
1 tablespoon minced parsley

Boil the potatoes and onion for 15 minutes in 1 cup of water. Add the seasonings and sour cream. (For a smoother consistency, purée the soup in a blender or food processor before adding the seasonings and cream, if desired.) Heat gently, then garnish with the parsley.

*Note: Thin store-bought sour cream with water until it is the consistency of heavy cream.

Corn Chowder

August 1929

SERVES 4 TO 6

3 tablespoons oil
2 tablespoons flour
2 onions, sliced
4 potatoes, cut into ¼-inch slices
2 cups fresh corn (or canned corn,
    well drained)
3 cups milk
salt and pepper

Heat the oil in a large skillet. Stir in the flour, and then carefully pour in 2 cups of water. Add the onions and potatoes and cook until the potatoes are soft. Add the corn and the milk and stir to combine. Cook for 10 minutes. Season to taste with salt and pepper.

    Served with graham bread and lettuce sandwiches, with apples for dessert.

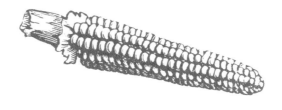

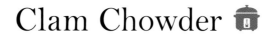

Clam Chowder

November 1928

SERVES 6 TO 8

6 slices bacon, diced
4 medium onions, diced
1 quart potatoes, peeled and diced
4 tablespoons butter
salt and pepper
3 cups fish stock or clam juice
1 quart shucked fresh clams, with
    their liquor reserved
1 cup milk
1 cup heavy cream
crackers, for serving

Fry the bacon, place it in the slow cooker, and fry the onion in the pan with the bacon drippings. Add the cooked onion to the slow cooker with the potatoes, butter, salt and pepper to taste, and fish stock or clam juice. Set the slow cooker to low and cook for 3 to 4 hours, until the potatoes are tender.

    When the potatoes are soft, add the clams and their liquor, the milk, and the cream. Cook until heated through, about 30 minutes to 1 hour. Season with salt and pepper to taste. Serve hot with crackers on top.

Cream of Potato Soup/Potato Chowder

August 1910, May 1918

The warming goodness of potato chowder garnished with bacon is the perfect lunch after a hard day of playing in the snow, while the pureed version works as an elegant first course to a table of dinner guests. Freeze batches of the chowder to reheat in a snap for a hearty meal on a cold night or to thaw and puree as a time-saver for future dinners.

SERVES 4 TO 6

---

6 large potatoes, peeled and diced
1 large yellow onion, chopped
1 tablespoon olive oil
4 cups chicken broth
salt and pepper to taste
4 slices bacon, chopped and fried, for garnish
chopped parsley or chives, for garnish

Place the potatoes in the slow cooker.

Heat the olive oil in a large skillet over medium heat and add the onion, stirring until it is soft and beginning to brown. Add the chicken broth and stir to deglaze the bottom of the pan, then add the mixture to the slow cooker. Set to low and cook for 4 hours. The soup may be served hot with the potatoes left in pieces and a garnishing of bacon and parsley or chives.

Variation: For a smooth soup, you may let the soup cool slightly and purée it in the blender, adding a drizzle of cream and parsley or chives to garnish. Taste for seasoning and add salt and pepper if desired.

Cream of Spinach Soup

SERVES 4

4 cups fresh spinach (or 1 package
    frozen spinach)
1 tablespoon butter
1 tablespoon flour
4 cups milk
salt to taste
½ teaspoon white pepper
¼ teaspoon grated nutmeg

Wash the spinach, drain, and put it in a saucepan with water to cover. Boil rapidly, uncovered, until tender, about 2 minutes, then drain in a colander, run cold water through it, and chop fine.

While the spinach is cooking, combine the butter and flour in a saucepan over low heat, slowly adding the milk and salt to taste. Season with the white pepper and grated nutmeg. Add the spinach and purée all the ingredients in a blender or food processor until smooth. Serve hot.

Cream of Tomato Soup

SERVES 4

1 pint (2 cups) canned tomatoes
1 slice from a large onion
1 small bay leaf
3 tablespoons butter
3 tablespoons flour
1 teaspoon salt
pepper
1 quart (4 cups) milk

In a medium-size saucepan, cook the tomatoes with the onion and bay leaf for 10 minutes. Remove the pan from the heat; strain and discard the liquid and remove the bay leaf. Keep the tomatoes hot.

As the tomatoes cook, make a thin white sauce. Melt the butter in a skillet, then add the flour, salt, and pepper (to taste). Stir to blend. Add the milk and stir until thickened. Keep hot.

Just before serving, pour the tomatoes into the white sauce. Serve at once. Always add hot tomatoes to hot milk rather adding milk to tomatoes.

Cream of Celery Soup 🍚

SERVES 4 TO 6

15 peppercorns
1 bay leaf
1 bunch celery
4 cups salted water or vegetable
    broth
2 tablespoons butter
salt and pepper
¼ to ½ cup heavy cream
chopped parsley, for serving

If desired, for easy removal after cooking, place the bay leaf and peppercorns in a muslin spice bag. Add the peppercorns and bay leaf to the slow cooker. Remove the tough outer strings from the celery, chop it, then add it to the slow cooker along with the water or broth. Set the slow cooker to low and cook the soup for 4 to 5 hours, until the celery is tender. Remove the peppercorns and the bay leaf. Allow the mixture to cool, then purée the celery and broth in a blender.

Reheat the soup in a large pot over the stove. When the soup is heated, stir in the butter, salt, and pepper, to taste. Remove the pot from the heat and add the cream, stirring to mix. Ladle the soup into bowls and garnish with the parsley.

Tomato Soup

August 1910

SERVES 4

---

1 medium yellow onion, quartered and thinly sliced

1 small carrot, peeled and minced (optional)

1 tablespoon butter

½ cup chicken broth, water, or beef broth

3 large, very ripe beefsteak tomatoes, about ¾ pound each, cored and cut into bite-size pieces

1 teaspoon salt

1 tablespoon sugar

1 teaspoon chopped dill, or more to taste

2 tablespoon heavy cream, or more to taste

In a skillet, sauté the onion (and carrot, if using) in the butter over low heat and cook until very soft, stirring occasionally. Deglaze the skillet with the broth and pour it all into the slow cooker. Add the tomatoes and all their juice, salt, and sugar. Set the slow cooker to low and cook for 4 hours. Pour the soup into a blender and purée. Pour the soup through a strainer if you do not like the occasional bit of tomato skin turning up in an otherwise smooth soup. Pour into a pot to reheat when ready to serve. Add the dill, stir in the cream, and allow the soup to warm but do not boil. Check for seasoning and serve.

A Stew of Distinction

September 1937

SERVES 6 TO 8

---

2 pounds veal or lean lamb shoulder

3 tablespoons lard

3 cups boiling water

4 carrots, cut into lengthwise pieces

1 small stalk celery, cut into 4-inch sticks

6 small white onions, peeled

6 medium-size potatoes, halved

1½ teaspoons salt

pepper

2 tablespoons chopped parsley

2 tablespoons flour, for making gravy

Wipe the meat with a damp cloth, then cut it into 2-inch cubes. Brown the meat in the lard in a Dutch oven. Add the boiling water, cover, and simmer for 45 minutes. Add the carrots, celery, onions, and potatoes, season with salt and pepper to taste, and cook for an additional 45 minutes. When the vegetables are done, use a slotted spoon to transfer the ingredients to a hot platter, piling the meat cubes in the center and arranging the vegetables in separate piles around the edge. Sprinkle the meat with the chopped parsley.

Serve the broth in a separate bowl. If desired, before removing the liquid from the heat, whisk in the flour as needed to thicken into a gravy.

Beef Stew

January 1924

This warming stew is perfect for a crowd (although it freezes wonderfully), and it can handle whatever you care to add to it. Delicate vegetables, like fresh peas, should be added half an hour before the stew is done. Heartier vegetables, like turnips, should be added with the carrots and onions. To thicken stews, use 2 tablespoons of flour for each pint of water used in making the stew.

SERVES 8

4 tablespoons butter

2 pounds beef stewing meat, cut into small pieces

2 cups chopped carrots

2 onions, thinly sliced

8 medium-size potatoes, cut in half and in half again

4 tablespoons flour

4 tablespoons cold milk (or water)

Optional ingredients: cooked rice, macaroni or hominy, cabbage, tomatoes, peas, beans, okra, turnips

Optional garnish: parsley, celery tops, or chopped sweet peppers

Heat the butter in a 4- or 6-quart soup pot or Dutch oven, then add the beef to brown in the butter. Add enough water to cook the meat and vegetables and cook the meat for 30 minutes. Add the carrots and onions and cook on low for 2 hours. Add the potatoes and cook for 30 more minutes.

Make a paste of the flour and the cold milk or water, adding enough cold liquid so the paste will pour. Add the paste to the stew, stir, and cook for 5 minutes to thicken.

Cooked rice, macaroni or hominy, cabbage, tomatoes, peas, beans, okra, and turnips may be added. Parsley, celery tops, or chopped sweet peppers add to the flavor.

Hasty-Tasty Stew

November 1936

SERVES 4 TO 5

---

2 strips salt pork (or bacon), diced
1 onion, minced
2 cups leftover cooked pork
1 cup diced celery
2 carrots, peeled and thinly sliced
2 potatoes, peeled and diced
1 (10¾-ounce) can condensed
    tomato soup
salt and pepper
Dumplings (see Chicken with
    Dumplings on pg. 79)

In a Dutch oven, fry the salt pork or bacon, then add the onion and the pork. When the pork is lightly browned, add the celery, carrots, potatoes, tomato soup, and 1 cup of water. (If you are using already-cooked vegetables, wait and add them with the dumplings.) Season as necessary with salt and pepper to taste, bring to a boil, and simmer for 15 minutes.

While the soup simmers, mix up the dumplings. Drop the dumplings in the soup, cover tightly, and cook for 15 minutes.

Limas and Lamb Stew 🍲

July 1930

SERVES 8

---

4 slices bacon, chopped
3 pounds lamb stew meat, trimmed
    of fat and cut into cubes
1 large yellow onion, thinly sliced
2 large carrots, peeled and cubed
4 cloves garlic, smashed and peeled
2 pounds new potatoes, peeled
    and cubed
1 cup dried lima beans, rinsed
1 cup chicken broth or water
salt and pepper
chopped fresh parsley, for garnish

Place the bacon in a large skillet and fry over medium-high heat. Add the lamb, onions, and carrots. Cook until the lamb is browned and the onions are softened. Add the garlic just before the onions are done. Place the lamb mixture in the slow cooker, as well as the potatoes and lima beans. Deglaze the skillet with the chicken broth or water and pour the contents of the skillet into the slow cooker. Season with salt and pepper, to taste. Set the slow cooker to low and cook for 5 to 6 hours until the meat is very tender. Make sure to keep an eye on the liquid, adding small additional amounts if necessary to keep the bottom from burning. Season to taste. Serve hot with chopped fresh parsley for garnish.

Ragout of Lamb and Early Vegetables: Substitute 1 pint small peeled pickling onions for the yellow onion (you may brown them quickly on the stovetop before adding to the slow cooker) and omit the lima beans. Substitute a few sprinklings of celery salt for some of the plain salt and add 1 to 2 tablespoons Worcestershire sauce to the pot. Half an hour before the stew is cooked, turn the heat to high and thicken the liquid with balls made of equal parts butter and flour. Stir in before re-covering the pot. Just before serving, add the grated rind and juice of 1 lemon. Season to taste and top with croutons.

Lentil Stew 🍚

February 1922

SERVES 4 TO 6

1 cup brown lentils, rinsed
½ cup barley, rinsed
2 large carrots, peeled and finely chopped
2 stalks celery, finely chopped
1 small onion, finely chopped
5 cloves garlic
1 teaspoon salt, or more
1 pound spinach, washed and chopped
butter, for serving
rice, for serving (optional)

Place the lentils, barley, carrots, celery, onion, garlic, and salt to taste in the slow cooker, and pour in 6 cups of water. Set the slow cooker to low and cook for 4 hours. In the last half an hour of cooking, add the spinach and stir.

Before serving, taste for seasonings, adding more salt and some pepper, as necessary. Ladle into bowls and top each serving with ½ tablespoon butter. Serve with rice, if desired.

Vegetable Stew 🍚

March 1930

SERVES 4

oil or bacon drippings, for pan
¼ cup chopped onion
½ cup chopped carrots
1½ cups cubed potatoes
1 cup lima beans
1 cup peas
½ cup chopped tomatoes
1 tablespoon butter
½ to 1 cup water or vegetable or chicken stock
salt and pepper
lemon juice
fresh herbs, for garnish
cooked rice, noodles, or cornbread, for serving

Heat the oil or bacon drippings in a large skillet and brown the onions and carrots. Add them to the slow cooker, followed by the potatoes, lima beans, peas, tomatoes, and butter. Pour in the water or stock. Cook for 2 to 4 hours, until all the vegetables are tender, stirring occasionally and making sure there is ample water at the bottom of the pot. Taste for seasonings and add salt, pepper, and lemon juice to taste. Garnish with fresh herbs. Serve over rice, noodles, or cornbread.

Version II: Follow the instructions above, replacing the vegetables with the following: 1 small onion, chopped; 2 sweet potatoes, cubed; 1½ cups green beans; 1 cup corn; 4 okra pods; 1 large tomato, chopped.

Version III: Follow the instructions above, replacing the vegetables with the following: 1 onion, chopped; ½ cup chopped carrots; 1 cup cubed potato; 1 cup chopped tomatoes; ½ cup chopped celery; ½ cup peas; ½ cup shredded cabbage.

Version IV: Follow the instructions above, replacing the vegetables with the following: ½ cup chopped onion; ¼ cup chopped celery; ⅓ cup chopped carrots; ½ cup cubed potato; 1½ cups chopped tomatoes; ½ cup chopped okra.

Brunswick Stew

March 1938

There are a couple competing origin stories for Brunswick Stew, but regardless of wherever or whenever it was actually created, it shows up all over menus in the Southeast. It always contains lots of veggies— particularly corn and tomatoes—and some sort of protein (nineteenth-century recipes called for squirrel). The process of coating the chicken in seasoned breadcrumbs and pan-frying before adding to the slow cooker adds immense flavor.

SERVES 10 TO 12

½ cup breadcrumbs
salt and pepper
1 stewing chicken (5 to 7 pounds)
    cut into pieces, skin removed
2 tablespoons olive oil
2 onions, sliced
4 potatoes, peeled and diced
1 pint lima beans, fresh
8 tomatoes, chopped
corn cut from 8 ears
lump of butter
¾ cup water or broth

Mix the breadcrumbs with salt and pepper and dip the chicken to coat.

Heat the olive oil in a large skillet over medium-high heat. Add the chicken and brown on all sides, then place it in the slow cooker. Add the onions to the skillet and cook until lightly browned, then add them to the slow cooker along with the potatoes, lima beans, tomatoes, corn, butter, and water or broth. Set the slow cooker to low and cook for 4 to 6 hours, until the chicken and vegetables are all very tender. Season to taste. Serve hot.

Vegetable Soup

August 1910, March 1918

Vegetable soup is a grand way to use whatever your garden happens to be producing, whether it's spring carrots and potatoes or fall squash and parsnips. It's bright, fresh, and filling no matter when you make it—and because it's done in the slow cooker, you can spend more time in your garden while it cooks!

SERVES 6

---

1 large yellow onion, chopped

2 tablespoons bacon drippings or olive oil

salt

8 carrots, peeled and chopped

4 stalks celery, chopped

3 garlic cloves, peeled and smashed

2 yellow-fleshed potatoes, such as Yukon gold, peeled and chopped

6 peppercorns

2 tablespoons chopped flat parsley

juice of 1 lemon

Sauté the onion in bacon drippings or oil with a little salt until it begins to soften. Add the carrots, celery, and garlic and sauté until the onion just begins to brown, about 5 minutes more. Add the mixture to the slow cooker along with the potatoes, additional salt to taste (about 2 teaspoons), peppercorns, and water to just fully cover the ingredients (about 6 cups). Set the slow cooker to low and cook for 4 hours, until the vegetables are done. If the broth is not flavorful enough, turn the slow cooker to high, remove the lid, and continue to cook for 30 minutes to evaporate the water and condense the flavors (if you are pressed for time, a faster way to bring out more flavor is to boil the soup in a pot on top of the stove). Just before serving, add the parsley and stir to mix. Squeeze in the lemon juice to taste—up to 1 whole lemon—and add salt and pepper as needed. Serve immediately.

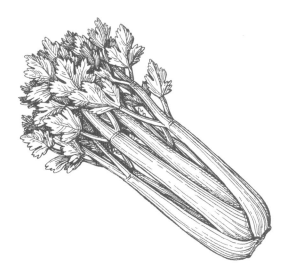

Black Bean Soup

January 1912

SERVES 6

1 large lemon

1 medium onion, chopped

6 stalks celery, chopped

1 tablespoon butter

1 pint (2 cups) dried black beans, soaked overnight in enough water to cover

2 tablespoons mustard

6 cups chicken broth (or water, for a vegetarian option)

salt and pepper

plain yogurt or sour cream, for serving

Juice the lemon and refrigerate the juice for use after the soup is cooked. Reserve the rind.

In a skillet, cook the onion and celery in the butter over medium-low heat until soft. Transfer the cooked vegetables to the slow cooker, then add the drained beans, mustard, the rind of the lemon, and the broth. Set the slow cooker to low and cook for 6 to 8 hours, until the beans are tender. Season with salt, pepper, and the juice of the lemon. Remove the lemon rind, then ladle about 2 cups of the soup into a blender, purée, and return to the slow cooker, mixing thoroughly. Serve with a dollop of plain yogurt or sour cream.

Chili con Carne

February 1926, December 1928

SERVES 6 TO 8

1½ pounds beef, such as chuck or brisket

2 cups pinto beans, soaked overnight in enough water to cover

2 cups crushed tomatoes

2½ teaspoons salt (or more, to taste)

2 tablespoons granulated or brown sugar

1 bay leaf

2 slices bacon, chopped

2 medium onions, quartered and thinly sliced

1 tablespoon ground cumin

1 tablespoon ground coriander

1 teaspoon moderately spicy chili powder (more or less, to taste)

½ teaspoon ground ginger

chopped cilantro, for garnish

Trim the beef of fat and slice it into ½-inch slices, then cut each slice in half lengthwise and slice it again to make short, thin pieces.

Drain the beans and place them in the slow cooker with the beef, tomatoes, salt, sugar, bay leaf, and 4 cups of water.

In a medium skillet, fry the bacon with the onions over medium-low heat until the onions are soft. Add the cumin, coriander, chili powder, and ginger to the skillet. Stir to mix, then add the mixture to the slow cooker. Stir it all together, making sure all the ingredients are covered with water. Set the slow cooker to low and cook for 8 hours. Serve over cooked rice and garnish with chopped cilantro if desired.

Breakfasts, Breads, and Biscuits

Sour Milk Griddle Cakes

1934

A griddle cake is just another way of saying pancake; the difference is the pan it's cooked in, whether it's a flat griddle or a frying pan. Either way, the addition of buttermilk makes these cakes extra fluffy when it reacts with the baking soda. If you're out of buttermilk, you can make a homemade sour milk by adding 2 tablespoons of lemon juice or vinegar to a glass measuring cup, then filling it to the 2-cup mark with milk. (If you need the extra ⅓ cup to get your batter to the right consistency, add 1 teaspoon of lemon juice or vinegar to it.)

SERVES 4

---

2 cups flour

2 tablespoons cornmeal

1 teaspoon salt

1 teaspoon baking soda

1 tablespoon sugar

2 to 2⅓ cups buttermilk

1 egg, beaten

2 tablespoons butter, melted, plus more for pan and for serving

In a large bowl, mix and sift together the flour, cornmeal, salt, baking soda, and sugar. Add the buttermilk, egg, and melted butter to the dry ingredients and mix well. Drop by large spoonfuls onto a buttered, hot griddle, flipping to cook on the second side when the first side is nicely browned.

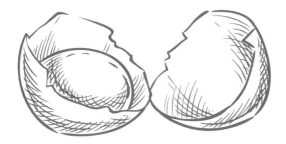

Rhode Island Johnny Cakes

November 1928

SERVES 4

2 cups white cap cornmeal*
1 teaspoon salt
milk
butter for greasing griddle
¾ cup huckleberries (optional)

Combine the cornmeal and salt in a medium-size bowl. Heat the teakettle to a jumping boil and pour boiling water over the meal a little at a time, beating vigorously until the meal is scalded but not thinned. Then add a little milk to the batter, until it is thinned to the consistency of a drop batter. Drop on a well-greased, hot griddle and cook like griddle cakes.

*Note: The meal used for these Johnny Cakes is made from white cap corn, stone ground by water power or wind because this method is slower and does not heat the meal. This is a special Rhode Island meal, which is now shipped in small quantities to many localities. It must be used quickly, as it soon deteriorates.

Huckleberry Johnny Cakes: Fold ¾ cup of huckleberries into the batter after thinning it with milk.

◆

Ham Omelet

April 1932

MAKES 1 OMELET

4 eggs
½ teaspoon salt
¼ teaspoon pepper
4 teaspoons butter, melted, plus
     more for the pan
4 tablespoons milk
½ cup chopped ham

Preheat the oven to 350°F.

Separate the egg yolks from the egg whites. Beat the egg whites until they form stiff peaks, then set aside.

Beat the yolks together, then add the salt, pepper, butter, and milk. Fold in the stiffly beaten egg whites and the chopped ham. Heat an oven-safe skillet over medium-high heat, then add butter. When the butter has melted, pour the egg mixture into the skillet and cook on low until the bottom of the omelet is golden brown and the omelet has puffed up. Transfer the skillet to the oven for 5 to 10 minutes to cook the top of the omelet. Crease the omelet through the center and fold it in half. Serve at once.

Variation: Instead of adding the ham to the egg mixture, put chopped ham, crisp diced bacon, dried beef, or sliced peaches between the folded-over omelet when it is done cooking.

Corn Scramble

May 1926

¼ pound bacon
2 cups corn kernels
6 eggs
1 cup milk
salt and pepper
toast or boiled noodles, for serving

Cut the bacon into pieces and fry it in a skillet with the corn. Drain all but 2 tablespoons of the bacon fat from the skillet.

In a medium-size bowl, beat the eggs slightly and add the milk, then pour the egg mixture into the skillet with the bacon and the corn and cook over low heat until creamy and thick, stirring all the time. Season with salt and pepper to taste and serve on toast or boiled noodles.

Eggs in a Potato Nest

May 1926

SERVES 6

1 small onion, chopped
butter
1 quart (4 cups) mashed potatoes*
6 eggs
paprika
2 tablespoons chopped parsley,
    for garnish

Preheat the oven to 350°F.

In a small skillet, cook the onion in butter until the onions are translucent.

Mix the potatoes with the onion and arrange the potato mixture in a greased 11 x 7-inch baking dish. Make 6 indentations in the potato layer. Drop an egg into each indentation. Sprinkle the eggs with paprika and bake for about 15 minutes, until the eggs are set. Garnish with chopped parsley.

*Note: Leftover potatoes may be used if enough hot milk to make them soft and creamy is added.

Baking Powder Biscuits

March 1931

Any Southern cook worth their salt pork will tell you the key to good biscuits is temperature. For the fluffiest biscuits, pop your butter or shortening and milk in the fridge for at least half an hour. Work the chilled butter or shortening quickly into the flour mixture without overprocessing and blend the wet and dry ingredients until they're the consistency of cottage cheese. Straight-from-the-oven biscuits make a great base for soaking up sauces, accompanying a plate of fried chicken and greens, or topping with Sausage Gravy (see page 76) for breakfast.

MAKES 10 TO 12 BISCUITS (USING A 2-INCH CUTTER)

---

2 cups flour
4 teaspoons baking powder
1 teaspoon salt
4 tablespoons butter or shortening
¾ cup milk

Preheat the oven to 400°F.

Measure and sift the flour, baking powder, and salt together; work in the butter or shortening either lightly with your fingertips or by cutting it in with two spatulas or knives. Add the milk all at once. Stir rapidly for a few seconds, turn out onto a lightly floured board, and knead vigorously for about half a minute. Pat or roll the dough to a ½- to ¾-inch thick. Cut the biscuits with a 2-inch cutter, transfer to a baking sheet (or to the top of a casserole), and bake for 12 minutes.

Orange Biscuits

1934

MAKES 10 TO 12 BISCUITS (USING A 2-INCH CUTTER)

2 cups flour
4 teaspoons baking powder
1 teaspoon salt
4 tablespoons butter or shortening
½ cup orange juice, plus more
    for soaking sugar cubes
¼ cup milk
12 sugar cubes
grated orange rind

Preheat the oven to 450°F.

Measure and sift the flour, baking powder, and salt together; work in the butter or shortening either lightly with your fingertips or by cutting it in with two spatulas or knives. Add the orange juice and milk all at once. Stir rapidly for a few seconds, turn out onto a lightly floured board, and knead vigorously for about half a minute. Roll out the dough to ⅓-inch thick, cut, and transfer to a baking sheet. Dip each sugar cube in orange juice long enough to absorb some of the juice but not long enough to dissolve. Place a sugar cube on top of each biscuit, and sprinkle with the grated orange rind. Bake for 10 to 12 minutes.

Milk Hoecake

SERVES 4

2 cups cornmeal
1 scant teaspoon baking soda
1 scant teaspoon salt
1 egg, beaten
enough fresh clabber* or
    buttermilk to make a cakelike
    batter
bacon drippings (optional)

In a large bowl, mix the cornmeal, baking soda, and salt. Stir in the egg, then pour in enough clabber or buttermilk to create a cakelike batter. Mix until just combined. If desired, bacon drippings may be added to make a richer texture. Cook like pancakes on a greased griddle uncovered on top of the stove.

Variation: When baked in muffin tins, this recipe makes delicious muffins or " egg bread." Beat 1 egg with 1 tablespoon water and brush on top of the "breads" before baking.

*Note: *Clabber* is raw milk that has soured and thickened—an old-fashioned farm product.

Knedliky (Bohemian)

February 1928, contributed by Mrs. M.V., Ohio

MAKES ABOUT 3 DOZEN DUMPLINGS

---

4 cups flour
1 tablespoon salt
½ teaspoon baking powder
1¾ cups milk
1 egg
2 slices bacon, chopped
½ onion, sliced

Set a large pot of water on the stove to boil.

Mix together the flour, salt, baking powder, milk, and egg, making a stiff dough that will hold the spoon upright.

When the water is boiling, dip the spoon first in the boiling water, then use the spoon to scoop some dough and drop it into the boiling water. When all the dough has been dropped in the water, cover the pot and boil it for 5 minutes, then stir the dumplings from the bottom. Replace the lid and boil for another 25 minutes. Remove one dumpling from the pot and check to see if it is done on the inside. If it is not ready, let them continue to boil. Once the dumplings are cooked inside, drain and place the in a bowl.

In a skillet, fry the bacon and onion, then pour the contents of the skillet over the bowl of knedliky. Serve at once.

Spoon Corn Bread

November 1911

SERVES 6

---

1 tablespoon melted butter or oil,
   plus extra for greasing the
   slow cooker
2 cups milk
½ cup fine-ground cornmeal
2 eggs
1 teaspoon baking powder
½ teaspoon salt
1 to 2 tablespoons sugar (optional)

Butter the inside of the slow cooker. Add the milk, melted butter, cornmeal, eggs, baking powder, salt, and sugar, if using, to the slow cooker and whisk very well to incorporate. Make sure that the eggs and baking powder especially are beaten in. Set the slow cooker to low and cook for about 3 hours until just set. To serve, spoon onto plates right from the pot, nice and hot.

Corn Bread

March 1921

This is a classic American dish with roots in many directions: south to the Aztecs and east to England. Traditionally, it is soft and light thanks to the addition of baking soda. As a rule it also generally eschews the use of sugar, although contemporary corn bread lovers who have grown accustomed to more sweetish stuff may wish to add a bit of sweetener (as does this recipe).

SERVES 8 TO 12

---

1 cup cornmeal
1 cup flour
1 tablespoon sugar
1 teaspoon baking soda
1 teaspoon salt
1 tablespoon shortening
1½ cups buttermilk
1 egg, well beaten

Preheat the oven to 400°F.

In a large bowl, sift together the cornmeal, flour, sugar, baking soda, and salt. Work in the shortening either lightly with your fingertips or by cutting it in with two spatulas or knives. Add the buttermilk and mix to a medium batter. Whip in the egg, then pour into an 8- or 9-inch square baking dish and bake for 20 to 25 minutes.

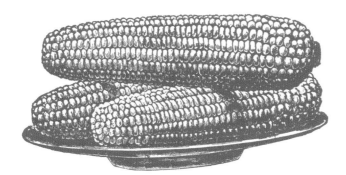

German Kuchen (Coffee Cake)

April 1938

MAKES 2 LOAVES (12 SLICES EACH)

1 package active dry yeast
¾ cup granulated sugar, divided
¼ cup lukewarm water (90°F to 110°F)
1 cup milk
3½ cups flour, sifted before and after measuring, divided
1 teaspoon salt
1 egg, slightly beaten
½ teaspoon nutmeg
½ cup raisins
¼ cup shortening, melted
butter, for greasing the pans

For the Topping:
1½ tablespoons butter, softened
2 tablespoons granulated sugar
1 tablespoon brown sugar
½ teaspoon cinnamon (optional)

In a large mixing bowl, dissolve the yeast and 2 tablespoons of the granulated sugar in the lukewarm water.

Scald the milk and allow it to cool until it is lukewarm, then add it to the dissolved yeast and sugar mixture. Add half of the sifted flour and beat thoroughly. Cover, and allow the sponge to rise in a warm place until it is full of bubbles, about 45 minutes.

Add the remainder of the sugar, the salt, the egg, the nutmeg, the raisins, and the melted shortening. Add the remainder of the flour gradually and beat thoroughly after each addition. Let the dough stand for 10 minutes.

Turn out the dough onto a lightly floured board and knead until it is smooth and elastic. Place the dough in the bowl, cover, and let it rise until it doubles in size, about 1½ hours.

Grease two 9 x 5-inch loaf pans. Shape the dough into 2 loaves and put them in the prepared pans. Let the loaves rise until they are light, about 45 minutes.

Preheat the oven to 400°F.

For the topping, spread the top of each risen loaf with the soft butter, then sprinkle with the granulated sugar, brown sugar, and cinnamon, if using. Bake for 30 minutes. Remove the loaves from the pans and allow to cool before storing.

Steamed Brown Bread

July–August 1921

MAKES 2 LOAVES (12 SLICES EACH)

---

butter for greasing the pan
1½ cups graham flour
2 cups cornmeal
1 tablespoon baking powder
1½ teaspoons salt
⅓ cup currants
⅔ cup raisins
2 cups milk
⅔ cup molasses

Preheat the oven to 325°F and bring a large pot of water to a boil. Grease the bottom and sides of two 9 x 5-inch loaf pans.

Mix together the flour, cornmeal, baking powder, salt, currants, and raisins. Add the milk and molasses and beat well. Pour the batter into the prepared loaf pans. Fill each pan slightly over half full with batter. Cover the pans with foil.

Place the loaf pans in a large, high-sided roasting pan, then pour the boiling water into the roaster, until it reaches one-third up the side of the pan. Place the pan in the oven and steam for 3 hours.

Orange Rolls

December 1932

MAKES 12 ROLLS

---

butter for greasing the pan
2 cups flour
2 teaspoons baking powder
½ teaspoon salt
1 tablespoon shortening
1 egg
½ cup milk
1 cup unsalted, creamed butter
12 orange segments, dipped in sugar
3 tablespoons butter, melted

Preheat the oven to 350°F. Grease a 9 x 13-inch baking pan.

Sift the flour, baking powder, and salt together. Add the shortening, mixing with a fork. Beat the egg slightly and add it to the mixture, followed by the milk. Roll the dough into an oblong large enough to cut out twelve 3-inch circles, about ¼ inch thick. Cut the dough into 3-inch circles; spread with the creamed butter, and place a segment of fresh orange coated with granulated sugar over half the circle. Fold over the other half to completely cover the orange and pinch the edges together. Place the rolls in the prepared baking pan and bake for about 20 minutes. Just before removing, brush the tops with the melted butter.

Cheese Straws

January 1934

Easy to whip up and impossible to resist, these cheese straws look as appetizing on the kitchen table awaiting hungry children after school as they do on the cocktail table for Saturday night drinks with the neighbors. The farmer's wife would have most likely used cheddar, but if you're feeling adventurous, use any cheese you like, as long as it can be grated easily and melts nicely. Pro tip: make more than you think you'll need because they disappear fast.

MAKES ABOUT 1 DOZEN STRAWS

---

butter for greasing the pan
½ teaspoon salt
1½ cups sifted flour
½ cup lard
3 to 4 tablespoons ice water
½ cup grated Cheddar or Monterey
   Jack cheese

Preheat the oven to 475°F. Lightly grease a cookie sheet.

In a large bowl, add the salt to the flour and cut in the lard with a dough blender, sharp-tined fork, or your fingertips until the pieces are the size of small peas. Add a little water at a time, mixing with a fork lightly until it can be shaped into a ball. Roll out the dough, being careful not to use too heavy a hand; use a light, patting touch. Spread half of the rolled dough with the grated cheese; fold over and roll again. Repeat 3 or 4 times. Cut into strips about ½ wide and 5 or 6 inches long, twist, and bake for 10 to 12 minutes.

Bran Muffins

October 1927

MAKES 1 DOZEN MUFFINS

---

butter for greasing the pan
2 tablespoons shortening
¼ cup sugar
1 egg
1 cup bran
1 cup flour
½ teaspoon salt
½ teaspoon baking soda
1 teaspoon baking powder
1 cup buttermilk

Preheat the oven to 375°F. Grease the cups of a 12-cup muffin pan or line them with paper liners.

In a large mixing bowl, cream together the shortening and sugar; add the egg and bran. In a small bowl, sift together the flour, salt, baking soda, and baking powder. Add the flour mixture to the large mixing bowl, followed by the buttermilk. Pour the batter into the prepared muffin pan and bake for 20 minutes.

Variation: To substitute regular milk for buttermilk, omit the baking soda and use 2 teaspoons of baking powder instead.

Sour Cream Muffins

May 1934

MAKES 1 DOZEN MUFFINS

---

butter for greasing the pan
2 cups sifted flour
1 teaspoon baking powder
½ teaspoon baking soda
2 tablespoons sugar
½ teaspoon salt
1 egg
1 cup sour cream

Preheat the oven to 425°F. Grease the cups of a 12-cup muffin pan or line them with paper liners.

In a large bowl, sift together the flour, baking powder, baking soda, sugar, and salt.

In a small bowl, beat the egg until it is foamy, then stir in the sour cream. Pour the wet ingredients, all at once, into the dry and stir vigorously until the dry ingredients are just dampened. The batter should not be entirely smooth. Fill the prepared muffin tins two-thirds full with as little extra stirring as possible. Bake for 20 minutes.

Raisin Muffins

May 1934

MAKES 1 DOZEN MUFFINS

butter for greasing the pan
2 cups sifted flour
2 teaspoons baking powder
2 tablespoons sugar
½ teaspoon salt
½ cup raisins
1 egg
1 cup milk
3 tablespoons butter, melted

Preheat the oven to 425°F. Grease the cups of a 12-cup muffin pan or line them with paper liners.

In a large bowl, sift together the flour, baking powder, baking soda, sugar, and salt. Mix in the raisins.

In a small bowl, beat the egg until it is foamy, then stir in the milk and butter. Pour the wet ingredients, all at once, into the dry and stir vigorously until the dry ingredients are just dampened. The batter should not be entirely smooth. Fill the prepared muffin tins two-thirds full with as little extra stirring as possible. Bake for 20 minutes.

Variation: Substitute ½ cup chopped dates or nuts for the raisins, mixing them into the dry ingredients before the liquids are added.

Potato Muffins

May 1918

MAKES 1 DOZEN MUFFINS

4 tablespoons butter, plus more
    for greasing the pan (if using)
2 tablespoons sugar
1 egg, well beaten
1 cup mashed potato
2 cups flour
1 tablespoon baking powder
1 cup milk

Preheat the oven to 350°F. Grease the cups of a 12-cup muffin pan or line them with paper liners.

In a large mixing bowl, cream together the butter and sugar; add the egg and potato and mix thoroughly. In a small bowl, sift together the flour and baking powder. Stir the sifted dry ingredients into the wet ingredients alternating with the milk. Bake in the prepared muffin tins for 25 to 30 minutes.

Blueberry Muffins

August 1923

When blueberries are in season, who can resist them? These simple-to-make muffins will reward your taste buds! The delicate berries are dusted with flour to help suspend them in the batter (rather than sinking to the bottom) and folded in last to keep them plump and whole. When you've picked more berries than you know what to do with, make extra batches of these muffins and freeze them for that burst of summer bliss all year long.

MAKES 1 DOZEN MUFFINS

---

3 tablespoons butter, plus more
    for greasing the pan (if using)
1½ cups sifted flour, divided
1 cup blueberries
½ cup sugar
2 eggs, beaten
1 tablespoon baking powder
½ teaspoon salt
1 cup milk

Preheat the oven to 400°F. Grease the cups of a 12-cup muffin pan or line them with paper liners. Sprinkle about a tablespoon of the flour over the blueberries and set them aside.

In a large mixing bowl, cream together the butter and sugar; add the eggs.

In a small bowl, sift together the remaining flour, baking powder, and salt. Stir the dry ingredients into the wet ingredients alternating with the milk. Fold in the berries last, being careful not to crush them. Fill the prepared muffin cups about half full and bake for about 20 minutes.

Cranberry Muffins

November 1933

MAKES 1 DOZEN MUFFINS

---

butter for greasing the pan
2 cups flour
2½ teaspoons baking powder
½ teaspoon salt
2 tablespoons sugar
½ cup ground cranberries
1 egg
1 cup milk
2 tablespoons butter, melted

Preheat the oven to 400°F. Grease the cups of a 12-cup muffin pan or line them with paper liners.

In a large bowl, sift together the flour, baking powder, salt, and sugar. Mix in the cranberries.

In a small bowl, beat the egg until it is foamy, then stir in the milk and butter. Pour the wet ingredients, all at once, into the dry and stir vigorously for about 3 seconds, mixing only until the dry ingredients are just dampened. Fill the prepared muffin tins a little over one-third full. Bake for 20 minutes.

Scotch Scones

March 1933, contributed by B.W., Massachusetts

MAKES 8 SCONES

---

2 cups flour
2 teaspoons baking powder
2 teaspoons sugar, plus more
    for topping
¾ teaspoon salt
4 tablespoons butter
2 eggs
⅓ cup milk

Preheat the oven to 450°F.

Sift together the flour, baking powder, sugar, and salt. Work in the butter either lightly with your fingertips or by cutting it in with a dough blender or two spatulas or knives.

Crack the eggs into a small bowl and reserve a tablespoon of the egg white. Beat the rest of the eggs, add the milk, and beat again. Add the egg mixture to the dry ingredients and mix lightly and quickly.

Toss the dough onto a floured board, roll out to a 1-inch thickness, and cut the dough into triangles* with a knife. Transfer the triangles to a baking sheet, brush the tops with the reserved egg white, sprinkle with sugar, and bake for 10 to 15 minutes.

*Note: If you prefer, you may cut the dough into squares and folded them over to form three-cornered shapes.

Banana Loaf

March 1939, contributed by Mrs. E.O. Park

MAKES 1 LOAF (12 SLICES)

4 tablespoons butter, plus more for greasing the pan

2 cups sifted flour

1 teaspoon baking soda

½ teaspoon salt

1 cup nut meats

1 cup sugar

1 egg

3 bananas, mashed

Preheat the oven to 350°F. Thoroughly grease a standard-size loaf pan.

In a small bowl, sift together the flour, baking soda, and salt. Stir in the nuts.

In a large mixing bowl, cream together the butter and sugar, add the egg and bananas, and blend well. Add the dry ingredients to the batter and stir just until the flour is dampened. Pour the batter into the prepared loaf pan and bake for 1 hour.

Whole Wheat Bread

1934

MAKES 3 LOAVES

1 quart (4 cups) milk

⅓ cup brown sugar or honey

6 tablespoons butter, plus more for greasing the pans

2 tablespoons salt

2 (0.6-ounce) cakes compressed yeast*

¼ cup lukewarm water (90°F to 110°F)

6 cups whole-wheat flour

3 cups white flour, plus more for kneading

2 tablespoons butter, melted

Scald the milk in a double boiler with the sugar, butter, and salt. Cool to lukewarm.

In a large bowl, dissolve the yeast in the lukewarm water, then add the milk. Add enough whole-wheat flour to make a batter. Beat thoroughly; then add the rest of the whole-wheat flour and the white flour to knead. The dough should be of a softer consistency than for white bread, but not actually sticky.

Turn the dough out onto a floured surface and knead for 10 to 15 minutes. Grease the inside of a large bowl and roll the dough around inside. Cover the bowl and set it in a warm place (80°F to 85°F) to let the bread rise until it doubles in bulk.

Knead the dough down slightly without adding more flour. Cover the dough and let it rise again until it doubles in bulk.

Thoroughly grease 3 bread pans. Form the dough into 3 loaves and transfer them into the prepared bread pans. Brush the tops of the loaves with the melted butter. Cover and let rise until double in bulk.

Preheat the oven to 400°F. Bake until a golden brown.

*Note: If you don't have compressed (fresh) yeast on hand, you can substitute 2 packages active dry yeast.

Butterhorn Rolls

April 1937

These lightly sweet crescent-shaped rolls are sure to impress any guest—but they're equally suitable for a weeknight dinner. In a pinch, they can do double duty as a dessert; once they've cooled, give them a light drizzle of confectioners' sugar mixed with just enough water, lemon juice, or maple syrup to form a thin glaze.

MAKES 16 ROLLS

---

1 cup milk

½ cup plus 2 tablespoons sugar, divided

1 (0.6-ounce) cake compressed yeast*

1 cup lukewarm water (90°F to 110°F)

7 to 8 cups sifted flour, divided

½ cup butter or shortening

6 egg yolks

1 tablespoon salt

soft butter, for spreading on rolls before baking

1 egg, beaten with 1 tablespoon cold water

Scald the milk in a double boiler with 2 tablespoons of the sugar and cool to lukewarm.

In a large bowl, dissolve the yeast in the warm water. Pour in the milk mixture, then add 3 cups of flour to make a spongy batter. Beat the batter, then let it stand until light.

In a small bowl, cream the butter and remaining ½ cup sugar. Add the egg yolks and beat until light and fluffy. Add the butter mixture, the remaining 3 to 4 cups flour, and the salt to the spongy batter in the large bowl. Knead lightly, cover, and let the dough stand in a warm place until it doubles in bulk.

Grease a large baking sheet. Divide the dough into 3 pieces, then roll out each piece into a ⅓-inch-thick round. Spread the rounds with soft butter, then cut each round into pie-shaped pieces. Beginning at the large end of a piece of dough, roll up each section with the point at the top. Place the rolls on the greased baking sheet, brush with the egg mixture, cover, and let stand until double in bulk.

Preheat the oven to 425°F. Bake for 20 minutes.

*Note: If you don't have compressed (fresh) yeast on hand, you can substitute 1 package active dry yeast.

Sweet Rolls

April 1938

MAKES 16 ROLLS

---

1 cup milk

1 cup lukewarm water (90°F to 110°F)

2 packages active dry yeast

½ cup butter

⅔ cup sugar

1 teaspoon salt

2 eggs, beaten

juice and zest of ½ lemon

⅛ teaspoon nutmeg

7 cups sifted flour, divided

Scald the milk in a double boiler and cool to lukewarm.

In a small bowl, pour the lukewarm water over the yeast, stir, and let it stand for 10 minutes.

In a medium-size bowl, cream together the butter, sugar, and salt.

In a large bowl, combine the beaten eggs, lemon juice, lemon zest, and nutmeg. Pour in the warm milk and the yeast mixture, then stir in 3 cups of the flour and beat until smooth. Add the butter-sugar mixture and enough flour to make a soft dough.

Turn the dough out onto a floured surface and knead until smooth, but keep the dough as soft as can be handled without being sticky. Let the dough rise in a cozy, warm place until it doubles in size.

Preheat the oven to 400°F. Shape the dough into 16 rolls at once. Bake for about 20 minutes.

Ice Box Rolls

1934

MAKES 96 SMALL ROLLS

---

1 quart (4 cups) milk

1 (0.6-ounce) cake compressed yeast*

¼ cup lukewarm water (90°F to 110°F)

1 cup mashed potatoes

½ to ¾ cup sugar

¾ cup shortening, melted

1 teaspoon baking powder

1 teaspoon baking soda

1 tablespoon salt

2¾ cups flour

Scald the milk in a double boiler and cool to lukewarm.

Dissolve the yeast in the warm water.

Mix together the mashed potatoes, sugar, shortening, baking powder, baking soda, salt, milk, and yeast mixture, then add enough of the flour to make a thin batter or sponge. Let the dough rise until it is full of bubbles. Add the rest of the flour to make a dough as stiff as would be desirable for Parker House rolls. Knead thoroughly. Transfer the dough to a large container with a cover; grease the top of the dough and close the lid. Put the dough in the ice box for at least 24 hours before using. This mixture will keep for several days.

When you are ready to bake, take out as much dough as you need and allow it to stand in a warm room for about 2 hours. Form the dough into rolls, then let the rolls rise on the pan for 1 hour. In the meantime, preheat the oven to 425°F. Bake the rolls for about 20 minutes.

*Note: If you don't have compressed (fresh) yeast on hand, you can substitute 1 package active dry yeast.

Meat, Fish, and Poultry

Meatballs

March 1927

SERVES 4
---

3 slices dry bread
1 quart (4 cups) canned crushed
    tomatoes
salt and pepper
1 pound ground sausage, pork,
    or beef
1 large onion, grated

Use a grater, blender, or food processor to make crumbs from the dry bread.

Put the tomatoes in a large saucepan or Dutch oven, season to taste with salt and pepper, and heat over medium heat.

In a large bowl, mix together the ground meat, onion, and breadcrumbs. Form into balls about the size of walnuts and drop into the pot with the tomatoes. Boil for about 20 minutes.

Meatloaf

April 1930

SERVES 6 TO 8
---

2 strips bacon or salt pork
2 pounds ground beef
⅝ cup tapioca, uncooked
2 cups canned tomatoes
½ small onion, chopped
2½ teaspoons salt
¼ teaspoon pepper
small onions, for garnish
radishes, for garnish
parsley, for garnish

Preheat the oven to 350°F.

Dice the bacon or salt pork and fry out the fat in a small skillet. In a large bowl, combine both the bacon and the drippings with the ground beef, tapioca, tomatoes, onion, salt, and pepper. Mix thoroughly, then transfer to a 9 x 5-inch loaf pan and bake for 45 to 60 minutes. Serve hot or cold with a garnish of small onions, radishes, and parsley.

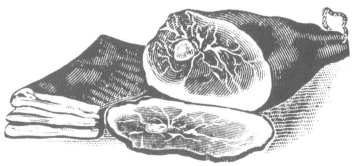

Hamburger Casserole

February 1935, contributed by Mrs. J.B.R., New Jersey

SERVES 4 TO 6

1 pound ground beef

1 egg, beaten

½ cup breadcrumbs

½ teaspoon salt

¼ teaspoon pepper

¼ teaspoon poultry seasoning

½ cup milk, divided

3 or 4 raw potatoes, thinly sliced

2 onions, thinly sliced

¼ cup milk

Preheat the oven to 325°F.

In a large bowl, thoroughly mix the ground beef, egg, breadcrumbs, salt, pepper, poultry seasoning, and ¼ cup of the milk.

Spread the potato slices in the bottom of an oblong 2-quart baking dish, then cover the potatoes with the meat mixture. Lay the onion slices on top and pour on the remaining ¼ cup milk, almost to cover. Bake for 1 hour.

Texas Hash

February 1921

SERVES 8

2 cups rice

4 quarts boiling water

4 small onions, sliced

2 pounds round steak, finely chopped

4 cups chopped tomatoes

2 teaspoons salt

½ teaspoon pepper

Preheat the oven to 400°F. Butter the bottom and sides of a 9 x 13-inch baking dish.

Cook the rice in the boiling water over low heat until soft, then drain.

In a large skillet, cook the onions, steak, tomatoes, salt, and pepper together for 20 minutes. Stir in the rice, then transfer the hash to the prepared baking dish and bake for 15 to 20 minutes.

Pot Roast 🍲

May 1933

Chuck roast is a slow cooker's best friend. That long, slow simmer in flavorful broth help soften the meat until it practically melts in your mouth. Use whatever sturdy vegetables you like—and omit those you don't. If you prefer a thicker, more stew-like broth, dredge the meat in flour before browning it, or smash a couple pats of butter with an equal measure of flour and add it to the slow cooker at the end of cooking.

SERVES 8 TO 12

---

3 to 4 pounds boneless chuck
    roast, trimmed of fat
2 tablespoons olive oil
salt and pepper
4 carrots, peeled, cut in half and
    then in 3-inch pieces
4 stalks celery, chopped
6 potatoes, peeled and quartered
1 medium turnip, peeled and
    chopped (optional)
2 large yellow onions, thinly sliced
1½ cups beef broth
¼ cup cider vinegar or red wine
chopped parsley or other fresh
    herbs, for garnishes

In a large skillet, brown the meat in the olive oil over medium-high heat and sprinkle with salt and pepper, turning the meat as you go. Place the roast in the slow cooker with the carrots, celery, potatoes, turnip (if using), onions, broth, and vinegar or wine. Set the slow cooker to low and cook for 7 to 9 hours, until the meat is very tender. Taste for seasoning. Garnish with chopped parsley or other fresh herbs, if desired.

Broiled Hamburgers

November 1938

SERVES 7

3 large, mild onions, divided
3 tablespoons butter
1 tablespoon water
1 pound lean ground beef
¼ cup ground suet or butter
1 cup soft breadcrumbs
1 tablespoon chopped parsley
salt and pepper
7 strips bacon

Preheat the oven to 350°F.

Peel and grate one of the onions. Strain the grated onion through a sieve and reserve 2 teaspoons of the juice. (You can store the remainder of the juice in a covered jar in the refrigerator.)

Cut the remaining 2 onions into seven ½-inch slices. Place them on the bottom of a flat baking dish with an oven-safe lid, add the butter and water, and cover. Put them in the oven to bake while you prepare the hamburgers.

Meanwhile, in a large bowl, mix the ground beef with the suet or butter, the breadcrumbs, the parsley, and the reserved onion juice. Add salt and pepper to taste. Knead the meat mixture into 7 flat cakes. Wrap each cake with a bacon strip and place each cake on one of the baked onion slices. Broil under direct heat for 5 minutes for each side, basting occasionally.

Variation: Cook on top of the stove, with sliced mushrooms sautéed in butter in place of the baked onions.

Curried Brisket with a Rice Border

November 1917

SERVES 8

2 pounds beef brisket
boiling water
2 cups finely chopped onion
2 teaspoons salt
2 tablespoons flour
2 teaspoons curry powder
1 tablespoon chopped celery
cooked rice, for serving

Wipe the meat with a paper towel, then cut into narrow strips. In a hot frying pan, sear the strips of meat on both sides, then put it in a large stew kettle and cover it with boiling water.

Brown the onions in the same pan used to sear the meat, then add them to the stew kettle. Season with the salt and simmer for 3 hours or until the meat is tender.

In a small bowl, mix the flour and the curry powder with a little cold water to make a paste. Add it to the meat, along with the celery. Bring the meat mixture to a boil, then simmer for 10 to 15 minutes. When the celery is tender, turn the curried brisket onto a platter, surround with a border of cooked rice, and serve.

Ground Steak, Italian Style (Meatballs)

November 1917

SERVES 8

2 pounds ground sirloin
2 tablespoons olive oil, plus extra
    for browning the meatballs
¼ cup stale breadcrumbs
1 teaspoon salt
pepper
⅛ teaspoon grated onion
2 eggs
2 (28-ounce) cans crushed tomatoes
1 onion, minced
2 cloves garlic, crushed
1 teaspoon salt
2 tablespoons butter
cooked macaroni, for serving

In a large bowl, mix the ground sirloin, olive oil, breadcrumbs, salt, pepper to taste, grated onion, and eggs. Form into small meatballs the size of walnuts.

In a large skillet, heat enough olive oil to cover the bottom of the pan, then add the meatballs and brown them over medium-high heat. Turn the meatballs several times to brown on all sides. Remove the meatballs with a slotted spoon and place them on a paper towel to drain.

While the meatballs are browning, mix the crushed tomatoes, onion, garlic, salt, butter, and 1 cup of water in the slow cooker. Add the meatballs once they are drained. Set the slow cooker to low and cook for 4 hours. Serve in the center of a platter with macaroni all around and sauce over all.

Hot Pot

March 1926

SERVES 4

1 pound shoulder of beef, cut into
    2-inch squares
2 tablespoons oil or butter
4 potatoes, peeled and thinly sliced
1 onion, cut fine
salt and pepper
water

Preheat the oven to 325°F.

In a large skillet, sear the bits of beef in the oil or butter. (Browning the meat gives the dish a better flavor.)

Butter a 2- or 3-quart baking dish and cover the bottom of the dish in alternate layers of meat and potato and onion, seasoning each layer with salt and pepper to taste. End with a layer of potato on the top.

Moisten the casserole with water, cover, and cook for 2 hours. If not brown enough, uncover for the last ½ hour.

Swedish Meatballs 🍲

May 1928

This beloved comfort food is easier to prepare than you might have imagined. The addition of breadcrumbs and grated potato to the meat mixture keeps the meatballs from falling apart as they simmer in the slow cooker, but it also prevents them from becoming too dense and heavy. Incorporating sour cream into the broth makes a richer sauce that will coat the noodles thoroughly.

SERVES 6

---

1 pound lean ground beef
½ pound lean ground pork
1 medium potato, grated
1 egg, beaten
¾ cup fine dry breadcrumbs
½ teaspoon pepper
1 teaspoon salt
½ teaspoon sugar
1 small onion, grated
2 to 3 tablespoons milk
3 tablespoons butter
1 cup beef broth
½ cup sour cream (optional)
¼ cup chopped parsley, for garnish
buttered egg noodles or boiled
    potatoes, for serving

In a large bowl, combine the ground beef, ground pork, grated potato, egg, breadcrumbs, pepper, salt, sugar, onion, and milk, stirring to mix well. Form the mixture into 1-inch balls.

In a large skillet, heat the butter over medium-high heat, then brown the meatballs in the butter. Drain the cooked meatballs on a paper towel, then place them in the slow cooker. Add the beef broth. Set the slow cooker to low and cook for 2 to 3 hours, until cooked through but not mushy. Be sure to stir occasionally to ensure that all sides of the meatballs are cooking in the broth so they will not dry out. Use a slotted spoon to transfer the meatballs to a bowl. Taste the broth for seasoning and stir in the sour cream, if desired. Pour a little or all of the sauce over the meatballs and garnish with the parsley. Serve over buttered egg noodles or boiled potatoes.

Two-Tone Meatloaf

July 1936

SERVES 10 TO 12

Part I:
1 pound ground veal
¾ pound ground fat pork
3 crackers, rolled into crumbs
1 tablespoon chopped onion
1½ teaspoons lemon juice
2 tablespoons cream
salt and pepper

Part II:
1 pound ground fresh pork
½ pound ground cured ham
2 eggs, beaten
½ cup breadcrumbs
½ cup ketchup
½ teaspoon salt
dash of pepper

Preheat the oven to 325°F.

For part 1, in a large bowl, combine the ground veal, ground fat pork, cracker crumbs, onion, lemon juice, cream, and salt and pepper to taste. Mix thoroughly.

For part 2, in another large bowl, combine the ground fresh pork, ground cured ham, eggs, breadcrumbs, ketchup, salt, and pepper. Mix thoroughly.

Mold the first mixture into a firm oval loaf, and over it put the second mixture in an even layer. Place the loaf on a sheet of parchment or wax paper and set it on a rack in an open roasting or dripping pan. Bake the meatloaf uncovered for 2 hours. Makes a 3-pound loaf.

Veal Casserole 🍲

February 1939

SERVES 8

6 tablespoons butter
1 small yellow onion, chopped
1 pound mushrooms, stemmed
    and sliced
2 pounds veal steak, cubed, or
    sirloin, cut into 1-inch-thick
    strips
1 teaspoon salt
1 teaspoon paprika
¼ cup water or chicken broth
1 cup sour cream, at room
    temperature*
buttered noodles, for serving

In a large skillet, melt the butter over medium heat. Add the onions and cook until just translucent. Add the mushrooms, then the meat, and stir until the meat has lost its pink sheen. Transfer the mixture to the slow cooker and add the salt, paprika, and water or chicken broth. Set the slow cooker to low and cook for 2 to 3 hours, until the meat is very tender. Before serving, stir in the sour cream and mix well to incorporate. Season to taste and serve hot over buttered noodles.

*Note: This dish is a take on two Franco-Russian classics: Beef Stroganoff and Veal Soblianka. Both dishes make use of meat, mushrooms, and sour cream. Since sour cream will break apart from long cooking, mix it into the sauce after cooking for best results.

Baked Ham with Pineapple

December 1927

SERVES 4

1 slice ham, 1½ inches thick
6 slices pineapple, juice reserved

Preheat the oven to 425°F.

Wipe the ham with a paper towel, then place it in a small roaster. Arrange the slices of pineapple on top of the ham. Pour in the juice from the can of pineapple, and add water if needed so the liquid comes half way up the side of the meat. Bake at 425°F to begin, then turn down the oven to 350°F and continue baking until ham is tender.

Ham and Sour Cream Casserole

1934

SERVES 4

2½ cups uncooked noodles
1 small onion, chopped
3 tablespoons butter, plus more
    for greasing the pan
1 pound cooked ham, cut into small
    pieces
2 teaspoons chopped parsley
3 eggs, beaten
½ teaspoon nutmeg
⅛ teaspoon pepper
2 cups sour cream
1 cup breadcrumbs

Preheat the oven to 350°F. Grease the bottom and sides of a large baking dish.

Following the package directions, boil the noodles in salted water until tender. Drain and set aside.

In a large skillet, brown the onion in the butter. Add the ham and parsley and remove the skillet from the heat. In a large bowl, beat together the eggs, nutmeg, pepper, and sour cream. Pour in the ham mixture, add the drained noodles, and mix. Transfer the mixture to the prepared baking dish and spread the breadcrumbs on top. Bake uncovered for 30 minutes or until set.

Slow Cooker "Baked" Ham

February 1923, contributed by Anna Coyle

A beautifully decorated platter of baked ham is the centerpiece for many family feasts, and this slow-cooker version has the added benefit of freeing up your oven for preparing all the delicious side dishes that accompany your meal. Should any ham remain after your feast, use leftover slices in sandwiches or fry them up to serve at breakfast.

SERVES 10

---

1 (5-pound) ham, with bone in
¼ cup brown sugar
cloves
1 cup apple cider
½ cup raisins (optional)

Rub the ham all over with the brown sugar, score the fat with a criss-cross pattern, and place a clove at each intersection of the scored lines. Place the ham in a slow cooker and add the apple cider. Set the slow cooker to low and cook for approximately 6 hours until the ham is tender. Add the raisins if desired and cook an additional ½ hour. Slice to serve.

Stuffed Pork Loin

1934

Pork loins make terrific weeknight meals. They're inexpensive and don't take long to cook when roasted at a high temperature. This recipe takes the lower-and-slower approach and only looks like a special-occasion dish. The small addition of pickles with the stuffing makes for a surprising pop of flavor throughout—don't skip them!

SERVES 6 TO 8

---

2 pounds pork loin
Sage Stuffing (see below)
2 tablespoons chopped pickles
flour
salt and pepper

Preheat the oven to 350°F.

Make the roast into a long, flat rectangle: Place the pork fat side down, then, with your knife parallel to the cutting surface and about ½ inch from the bottom of the roast, make a slice along the long side of the roast from one end almost the whole way to the other side. Roll open the pork, then make another cut, beginning ½ inch from the bottom again. Repeat until the meat is one flat piece.

Spread the stuffing over the pork and sprinkle on the pickles. Roll the meat up like a jelly roll and tie with twine. Sprinkle with the flour and salt and pepper to taste. Roast for 1 hour, basting occasionally.

Sage Stuffing

2½ cups bread cubes
1 cup beef or chicken stock
1 tablespoon powdered sage
salt and pepper
1 small onion, finely chopped
½ cup butter, melted, or sweet
    cream
2 eggs, unbeaten

Soak the bread in the stock. Add the sage and season well with salt and pepper, to taste. Add the onion, then stir in enough butter or cream to make the mixture moist in texture. Stir in the unbeaten eggs until incorporated.

Emergency Casserole

February 1933, contributed by Mrs. J.J.G., North Dakota

SERVES 6

2 tablespoons butter, plus more
    for topping
1 onion, thinly sliced
3 carrots, diced
1 slice bacon, cut into small pieces
2 cups diced potatoes
breadcrumbs
salt and pepper

Preheat the oven to 350°F.

    Place the butter in a baking dish. Add the onion, followed by a layer of carrots, a layer of bacon, and a layer of diced potatoes. Cover the top with breadcrumbs dotted with butter, salt, and pepper. Add enough water to cover the bottom of the dish and cover it tightly with foil. Bake for 30 minutes.

Baked Stuffed Apples

October 1932

MAKES 4 STUFFED APPLES

4 apples
½ pound mild or hot Italian
    sausage, casings removed

Preheat the oven to 300°F.

    Wash, pare, and core the apples. Spoon the sausage into the cored apples and place them in a baking dish. Bake until the apples are tender and the sausage is thoroughly cooked, about 1 hour.

Pork Chop Casserole

June 1927

SERVES 6

6 pork chops
½ cup uncooked rice, rinsed
1 (28-ounce) can tomatoes
1 small onion, chopped
salt and pepper

Preheat the oven to 350°F.

    Place the pork chops in a 9 x 13-inch baking dish. Add the rice, tomatoes, and chopped onion. Season with salt and pepper to taste and cover with water. Bake for 2 hours.

Roast Stuffed Spareribs

December 1934

SERVES 4

---

2 sides of spareribs
2 teaspoons salt, plus more for
    seasoning
1 teaspoon pepper, plus more for
    seasoning
2 tablespoons butter
1 onion, chopped
2 cups soft breadcrumbs
2 cups chopped cold cooked potatoes
1 teaspoon powdered sage
¼ cup flour
glazed onions and baked apples,
    for serving (optional)

Preheat the oven to 450°F. Trim the spareribs so they make two neat, rectangular pieces. Wipe the ribs with a damp cloth. Sprinkle the ribs with salt and pepper and sew together on one side, using a darning needle and some string.

Melt the butter in a skillet, add the onion, then the breadcrumbs and the potatoes. Cook until heated through and the breadcrumbs are lightly browned. Mix in the sage, salt, and pepper. Pile the stuffing lightly on one rib section and sew up the other side.

Add some salt and pepper to the flour, then rub the seasoned flour on the outside of the ribs. Place the ribs on a rack over a dripping pan or a roasting pan. Bake the ribs uncovered for 20 minutes, then reduce the oven temperature to 375°F and continue to cook until the ribs are well done, about an hour longer. To serve, carve between the ribs. If you'd like, serve the ribs on a platter with glazed onions and baked apples.

Escalloped Ham and Potatoes

February 1923

SERVES 6

---

6 medium-size potatoes
2 thick slices raw ham
2 tablespoons flour
¼ teaspoon pepper (optional)
2 cups milk

Preheat the oven to 375°F.

Pare and cut the potatoes into thin slices. Dredge the ham slices in flour and arrange the potatoes and ham in alternate layers in a 2-quart baking dish, ending with a slice of ham on top. Pepper, if used, should be sprinkled between the layers of ham and potato, but because of the salt in the ham, added salt will not be necessary. Pour in enough milk to reach to the top slice of ham. Bake for 45 minutes or until the ham is tender. Serve from the baking dish.

Sausage Pudding

April 1935

SERVES 4

---

2 eggs, separated
1 cup cooked oatmeal
1 cup milk
1 cup flour
½ teaspoon salt
2 teaspoons baking powder
12 sausage links
Sausage Gravy (optional, see below)

Preheat the oven to 400°F, and butter the bottom and sides of an 11 x 7-inch baking pan.

In a medium-size bowl, blend the oatmeal with the milk and the egg yolks. Sift in the flour, salt, and baking powder, beating well to combine, and then fold in the stiffened egg whites. Pour the mixture into the prepared pan and lay the sausage links across the batter. Bake for about 25 minutes, until firm and beginning to brown. Remove the pan from the oven and pour off the fat, reserving it for making Sausage Gravy, if desired. Return the pan to the oven and bake 5 minutes longer, until well browned. Drain off the fat again. Serve hot, plain or with Sausage Gravy.

Sausage Gravy

---

3 tablespoons sausage fat
4 tablespoons flour
½ teaspoon salt
2 cups milk

Heat the fat in a large skillet; add the flour and salt and whisk to blend. Whisk in the milk and stir until thickened.

Roast Pork and Apples

October 1922

SERVES 6

6 boneless pork loin chops, cut
    ¾-inch thick
2 tablespoons olive oil, divided
salt and pepper
1 medium onion, chopped
6 sour apples, peeled, cored, and
    chopped
4 cloves garlic, smashed
1 tablespoon brown sugar
¼ cup apple cider
nutmeg

Brown the pork chops in a large heavy-bottomed skillet in 1 tablespoon of the olive oil over high heat and sprinkle with salt and pepper. Place in one layer at the bottom of the slow cooker. Add 1 tablespoon olive oil to the skillet, then add onion and sprinkle with a little salt and pepper. Sauté the onion until soft. Add the apples and garlic and sauté an additional 2 minutes. Spoon the mixture over the pork chops, sprinkle the sugar over the mixture, and pour in the cider. Cook for 4 to 6 hours on low until tender (the exact time will depend greatly on the quality of meat used). A generous grating of fresh nutmeg just before serving enhances this dish.

Adouba

June 1938

SERVES 6

2 pounds boneless pork shoulder
1 tablespoon olive oil
¾ cup cider vinegar
1 teaspoon salt
dash of cayenne
spice bag with:
   1 teaspoon whole cloves
   1 teaspoon whole or ½ teaspoon
    ground allspice
   2 sticks cinnamon
   2-inch piece ginger
cooked rice, for serving

Cut the pork into squares and trim off the fat. Heat the olive oil in a skillet over high heat and brown the pork. Transfer the pork to the slow cooker and add the vinegar, salt, cayenne, and the prepared spice bag. Set the slow cooker on low and cook for 4 hours or until very tender. Serve with rice.

Chicken with Dumplings

February 1937

Different versions of this recipe call for "dumplings" of all stripes. For some, a biscuit dough is made and spoonfuls are dropped into the broth. This one rolls and cuts the dough, then drops them in; they'll puff up nice and fluffy. Any way you slice it, though, the flour on the dumplings adds body to the broth, making this one excellent comfort dish.

SERVES 6 TO 8

3½ pounds chicken
1 small onion, chopped
salt and pepper
1 large potato, peeled and diced
2 carrots, chopped
2 stalks celery, chopped
¼ cup chopped parsley
Dumplings (see below)

In a large Dutch oven, stew the chicken with the onion in water to cover until almost done. Add the salt and pepper to taste, the potato, the carrots, the celery, and most of the parsley. Boil for 10 minutes, then drop in the dumplings. Cover and cook for 15 minutes without lifting the cover. Garnish with the remaining parsley before serving.

Dumplings

---

2 cups sifted flour
1 tablespoon baking powder
½ teaspoon salt
1 tablespoon butter, plus extra
    for spreading over dough
1 egg, beaten
½ cup milk, plus more as needed

Sift together the flour, baking powder, and salt. Rub in the butter, then add the egg and milk to make a soft dough, mixing just until the dough forms a ball.

Smothered Chicken

February 1935

SERVES 4 TO 6

3 to 4 pounds chicken, cut into
    serving pieces
3 tablespoons flour, plus more
    for dredging
salt and pepper
1 tablespoon lard
1 tablespoon butter
1 (8.5-ounce) can cream-style corn
1 cup cream
1 teaspoon paprika

Preheat the oven to 350°F.

    Roll the pieces of chicken in flour seasoned with salt and pepper. In a skillet, heat the lard and butter and brown the chicken lightly. Remove the chicken to a baking dish, and then add the flour to the fat that remains in the skillet, stirring until smooth. Add the corn, cream, ½ teaspoon salt, and paprika to make a rich-colored gravy. Stir, and when smooth, pour over the chicken,* cover, and bake until tender, removing the cover for the last 20 minutes to allow the chicken to brown.

*Note: If the chicken is rather young and tender, bake it uncovered at 325°F instead.

Casserole of Fowl

October 1929

SERVES 4 TO 6

flour for dredging
salt and pepper
3 to 4 pounds chicken pieces, skinned
3 tablespoons olive oil
1 onion, thinly sliced
2 stalks celery, sliced
1 cup water or chicken broth
2 small potatoes, peeled and chopped
6 carrots, peeled and sliced
1 bay leaf
chopped parsley, for garnish

Mix some flour with some salt and pepper and dredge the chicken pieces in the flour mixture. In a skillet, brown the chicken pieces in the oil over high heat. Drain the chicken on paper towels and place it in the slow cooker. Add the onion and celery to the browning skillet and cook until soft; add salt and pepper to season, then transfer the onion and celery to the slow cooker. Deglaze the pan with water or chicken broth and add the contents of the pan to the slow cooker along with the potatoes, carrots, and bay leaf. Set the slow cooker to low and cook for 4 to 5 hours. A longer cooking time will result in chicken that is falling off the bone. Add seasonings to taste and serve garnished with chopped parsley.

Chicken Shortcake

April 1935, contributed by M. Cupp., New York

SERVES 4

For the Muffins:

2 tablespoons butter, melted, plus
    more for the pan
1 cup cornmeal
1 cup flour
1 tablespoon baking powder
½ teaspoon salt
1 egg, beaten
1 cup milk

For the Filling:

3 tablespoons butter, plus more
    for the skillet
6 tablespoons flour
1 teaspoon salt
2 cups milk
1 cup chicken stock
1½ cups diced cooked chicken
8 pieces thinly sliced ham, cooked

To make the muffins, preheat the oven to 425°F. Grease 8 cups in a muffin pan. In a large bowl, sift together the cornmeal, flour, baking powder, and salt. In a small bowl, combine the egg, milk, and melted butter, and pour the wet ingredients into the dry ingredients all at once. Stir just enough to dampen the batter. Fill each greased muffin cup two-thirds full, to make 8 muffins. Bake for 20 minutes.

To make the filling, melt the butter in a double boiler, then add the flour and salt, and blend. Add the milk and the stock and stir until smooth. Add the chicken to the gravy and heat through.

In a skillet, lightly brown the ham pieces.

Cut each of the muffins in half, removing their tops. Place a slice of cooked ham and a spoonful of chicken mixture on the bottom of each muffin, then replace the tops and cover with another spoonful of chicken.

Chicken Goulash

October 1929

SERVES 6 TO 8

---

1 whole 5- to 6-pound chicken
2 cups chopped tomatoes
2 teaspoons salt
6 small onions, chopped
1 small green pepper, chopped

Boil the chicken in water to cover until tender, 2 to 2½ hours. Remove from the heat to cool, then remove the bones from the stock and cut the meat into small pieces. Return the meat to the broth, add the tomatoes, salt, onions, and pepper, and simmer for 1 hour. Check the seasoning before serving and adjust as needed.

Southern Fried Chicken

March 1938

You won't get a better fried chicken recipe than from a Southern farmer's wife. Take note of the specific steps, but most importantly, pay attention to your oil; it should be between 350°F and 375°F. If it's too hot, the chicken will burn before it's fully cooked on the inside; if it's too cold, the chicken will become greasy. Be sure to serve this with the classic Baking Powder Biscuits (see page 40).

SERVES 3 TO 4

2½- to 3-pound young chicken
flour
peanut oil, lard, or vegetable fat,
    for frying*

Select a young spring chicken, about 2½ to 3 pounds. Dress and disjoint it, then pat it dry to prepare it for the pan. The chicken should be thoroughly chilled before it is used, several hours or overnight.

To prepare the chicken for frying, sprinkle the slightly moist chicken with flour. Heat a skillet and then fill it to 1½ inches deep with the fat of your choice. Add in just a few pieces of the chicken at a time so the pieces do not touch. Fry gently, turning once, until each piece is crusty brown on all sides, a characteristic of good Southern fried chicken. Drain the chicken on paper towels or brown paper.

*Note: After frying, strain the fat into a can or jar, where it can be used again and again if it is not overheated during use.

Lamb Stew

September 1937

SERVES 6 TO 8

2 pounds lean lamb shoulder or veal
3 tablespoons lard
3 cups boiling water
4 carrots, cut into lengthwise pieces
1 small stalk celery, cut into 4-inch sticks
6 medium-size potatoes, halved
6 small white onions, peeled
1½ teaspoons salt
pepper
2 tablespoons chopped parsley
flour (optional)

Wipe the meat with a damp cloth. Cut it into 2-inch cubes. Brown well in a kettle or Dutch oven containing hot lard. Add the boiling water, cover, and simmer for 45 minutes.

Add the carrots, celery, potatoes, and whole onions. Add the salt and the pepper, to taste, and cook for 45 minutes more. When the meat and all the vegetables are tender, remove them to a hot platter, piling the meat cubes in the center and arranging the vegetables in separate piles around the edge of the platter. Sprinkle the meat with the chopped parsley. Whisk in some flour to thicken the gravy, if desired; serve it in a separate bowl.

Lamb Curry

April 1926

SERVES 8

2½ pounds lamb for stew, cut into 1-inch pieces
2 tablespoons olive oil, plus more for sautéing
salt
2 medium onions, chopped
2 cloves garlic, smashed
2 to 3 teaspoons curry powder
8 green cardamom pods
1 teaspoon ground cumin
1 cup chicken broth or water
1 cup crushed tomatoes
½ cup shredded unsweetened coconut
½ cup raisins
cooked rice, for serving chopped
yogurt, for serving
fresh cilantro, for garnish

Trim the lamb of fat, then brown in a large skillet in the oil over high heat and sprinkle with a little salt. Remove the meat with a slotted spoon and place it in the slow cooker.

Drain the skillet of fat, then add the onions, garlic, and a little more olive oil, if necessary. Cook until the onions are soft and slightly brown. Add the curry powder, cardamom, and cumin and stir for several seconds to mix. Add the mixture to the slow cooker.

Deglaze the skillet with the chicken broth or water, add the tomatoes, and stir briefly. Add the tomatoes to the slow cooker. Set the slow cooker on low and cook for 4 to 5 hours until the meat is very tender. Add the coconut and raisins after 3 hours to preserve their flavor. Serve over rice with a dollop of yogurt and cilantro to garnish.

Chicken or Beef Curry: You may substitute beef or chicken for the lamb. Omit the crushed tomatoes for a simpler flavor.

Rabbit Curry: Clean (and skin) a young rabbit. Cut the rabbit into pieces as for frying. Fry in bacon fat until a light brown. Fry 3 sour apples and 2 onions, finely chopped. Add 1 teaspoon curry powder and soup stock, salt, and pepper to taste. Add all to the slow cooker and follow the instructions above for Lamb Curry. Serve hot over rice or boiled, buttered noodles.

Escalloped Tuna and Peas

August 1931, contributed by Mrs. G.R., Michigan

SERVES 4

2 tablespoons butter, plus more
    for greasing the pan
6 tablespoons flour
1 teaspoon salt
¼ teaspoon pepper
½ teaspoon celery salt
3 cups milk
1 cup cooked peas
2 cups canned tuna, drained and
    flaked with fork
Buttered Crumbs (see page 116)

Preheat the oven to 350°F. Grease the bottom and sides of a 2-quart baking dish. In a large skillet, melt the butter; add the flour, salt, pepper, and celery salt. Blend together with a wooden spoon, and then stir in the milk. Cook until thick. Add the peas and the tuna and mix well. Pour into the prepared baking dish, then cover with the buttered breadcrumbs. Bake for 20 minutes.

Fish Cakes

March 1937

SERVES 4 TO 6

6 potatoes, peeled
2 cups salt fish, cooked and
    finely chopped
2 tablespoons butter
¼ cup milk
1 egg
pepper
butter or oil, for frying

Boil the potatoes until tender, drain, and mash the potatoes together with the fish until very light and fine. Add the butter, milk, egg, and pepper to taste. Drop by spoonfuls into hot fat and fry until brown.

Scalloped Salmon and Noodles

October 1932

SERVES 12

---

2 pounds noodles

⅓ cup butter, plus more for
    greasing the pan

⅓ cup flour

1 teaspoon salt

¼ teaspoon pepper

3 cups milk

4 eggs

1 (16-ounce) can salmon, drained
    and flaked with a fork

¼ cup butter

1½ cups cracker crumbs, rolled fine

Preheat the oven to 350°F. Grease the bottom and sides of a 9 x 13-inch baking dish.

Cook the noodles in boiling salted water until tender. Drain.

Melt the butter in a skillet; add the flour, salt, and pepper and stir to blend. Add the milk and stir until thickened.

In a large bowl, add the eggs to the salmon and beat slightly. Add the noodles and the white sauce to the salmon and mix together. Transfer the salmon mixture to the prepared baking dish and cover it with the cracker crumbs. Bake until golden and heated through.

Vegetables

Glazed Carrots

January 1931

There just might be as many recipes for glazed carrots as there are types of carrots, but this is the one you'll want to make again and again. It's the cider syrup that sets it apart, as it cooks down to a sweet glaze while the carrots roast until they're browned and meltingly tender. You might not even need to serve dessert!

SERVES 4 TO 6 AS A SIDE DISH

½ cup apple cider
½ cup maple sugar (or brown sugar)
1 pound carrots, peeled

Preheat the oven to 350°F.

In a small saucepan, stir together the cider and sugar and boil, stirring consistently, until thickened. Set aside.

In a large stock-pot, boil the carrots until they are just tender, 10 to 15 minutes. Drain and cut the carrots lengthwise in halves or in quarters if they are large. Place the carrots in a single layer in a 9 x 13-inch baking dish, then cover them in the cider syrup. Bake until the carrots are brown, basting occasionally with the liquid. Serve the carrots in the syrup.

Carrot and String Bean Casserole

June 1937, contributed by N.F., Nebraska

SERVES 6 TO 8 AS A SIDE DISH

1 small onion, minced

⅓ cup butter

3 tablespoons flour

1 teaspoon salt

dash of pepper

2½ cups milk

1 cup grated cheese

2 eggs

3 cups cooked carrots

3 cups cooked green beans

1 cup Buttered Crumbs
   (see page 116)

Preheat the oven to 350°F.

In a medium-size saucepan, cook the onion in the butter until soft, then add the flour, salt, pepper, and milk and cook until thickened, stirring to keep the sauce smooth. Add the cheese, stir until melted, then remove the pan from the heat.

In a medium-size bowl, slightly beat the eggs, then whisk a few spoonfuls of the hot sauce into the eggs to bring up their temperature without causing them to cook. Once you've added enough of the heated sauce that the eggs are also warm, pour the eggs into the sauce and stir. Arrange the sauce, carrots, and green beans in layers in a 2-quart baking dish, then top with the buttered crumbs. Bake the casserole until the crumbs are brown.

Normandy Carrots 🍲

November 1931

SERVES 4 TO 6 AS A SIDE DISH

1 pound carrots, peeled, and thinly
   cut into 2-inch strips
   (about 2 cups)

¼ cup sugar

¼ cup vinegar

2 tablespoons butter

¼ teaspoon salt

Add the carrot strips, sugar, vinegar, butter, and salt to the slow cooker. Mix well. Set the slow cooker to low and cook for 3 to 4 hours (depending on the age and thickness of the carrots), until the carrots are tender all the way through.

Cauliflower au Gratin

June 1922

SERVES 2 TO 3 AS A MAIN DISH, 4 TO 6 AS A SIDE DISH

1 large head cauliflower
salt (for salting water)
1 cup grated cheese
1 cup Buttered Crumbs
    (see page 116)
2 cups White Sauce (see page 112)

Remove the leaves and the stalk from the head of cauliflower and soak it in cold, slightly salted water for 1 hour.

Boil a large pot of water. When the water is boiling, add about 2 tablespoons of salt. To ensure the head of cauliflower retains its shape, wrap it in a square of cheesecloth. Place the cauliflower in the boiling water and cook for 30 minutes.

Preheat the oven to 350°F.

Transfer the cauliflower to a shallow baking dish and remove the cheesecloth (if using). Sprinkle the cauliflower with the grated cheese and buttered crumbs and brown in the oven at for about 20 minutes. Remove the cauliflower from the oven, cover with the white sauce, and serve directly from the baking dish at the table.

Cauliflower in Tomato Sauce

October 1918

SERVES 4 TO 6 AS A SIDE DISH

1 large head cauliflower
1 small onion, peeled and thinly
    sliced
2 tablespoons olive oil
1 cup crushed tomatoes
fresh thyme, rosemary, or sage
    (optional)
salt and pepper to taste
chopped fresh parsley, for garnish

Cut the cauliflower into florets and parboil in salted water for 2 minutes (if you are strapped for time, you may skip this step). Drain and put in the slow cooker.

Meanwhile, cook the onion in the olive oil until it is lightly browned. Add it to the slow cooker, as well as the tomatoes and fresh herbs (if using), salt, and pepper, to taste. Set the slow cooker to low and cook for 2 to 3 hours, until the cauliflower is nicely tender. Check for seasonings, garnish with parsley, and serve alongside buttered bread.

Baked Spinach with Cheese

February 1935, contributed by H.R., Indiana

This crowd pleasing recipe is perfect for the next time you're entertaining friends for a casual get-together. If you're expecting a large group, double the recipe and heat up the second dish when the first one is nearly gone. Choose a cheese such as Colby, Havarti, or Monterey Jack that melts smoothly, and serve with grilled French bread, toast points, or pita chips—any delivery method sturdy enough to hold this rich dip without falling apart.

SERVES 4

---

2 tablespoons butter
2 tablespoons flour
1 cup milk
½ cup grated cheese
2 eggs, separated
2 cups chopped cooked spinach

Preheat the oven to 350°F.

In a medium-size saucepan, melt the butter, add the flour, and stir to blend. Add the milk and stir until thickened. Add the cheese and stir until the cheese is melted and the sauce is thick and smooth. Remove the saucepan from the heat.

Beat the egg yolks slightly, then spoon a little of the hot sauce into the eggs and stir. Pour the egg yolks into the sauce and stir, followed by the spinach.

Beat the egg whites until stiff, then carefully fold them into the mixture. Transfer the spinach mixture to a 1½- or 2-quart baking dish and bake for 30 minutes.

Sweet Corn Delicious

August 1929

SERVES 8 TO 10 AS A SIDE DISH

---

8 ears corn
4 tablespoons butter
2 cups milk
1 teaspoon salt
⅛ teaspoon pepper

Cut the corn from the cob and place it in a frying pan with the butter. Cook for 12 minutes (or less, if you prefer crisper corn), then add the milk, salt, and pepper. Serve as soon as the milk is hot.

Creole Green Corn

October 1920

SERVES 6 TO 8 AS A SIDE DISH

---

6 ears fresh corn
1 tablespoon butter or oil
1 red bell pepper, chopped
salt
1 small onion, minced (optional)
2 tomatoes, diced (optional)

Cut the corn from the cob and put in the frying pan with the butter or oil. Cook for 10 minutes, then add the chopped pepper and season with salt to taste. Stir in the onion and tomatoes, if using.

Corn Pudding 🍚

November 1912

SERVES 4 TO 6 AS A SIDE DISH

---

1 tablespoon butter, plus extra for
   greasing the slow cooker
2 heaping cups corn kernels,
   fresh or frozen
3 eggs
2 tablespoons sugar
1½ cups milk
large pinch of salt

Heavily butter the inside of the slow cooker. Add 1½ cups of the corn to the slow cooker; finely chop the remaining ½ cup corn and add it to the slow cooker as well. Mix the eggs, sugar, milk, and salt in a large bowl, then add it to the corn. Set the slow cooker to low and cook for 2 hours until just set. Serve hot.

Succotash

February 1922

SERVES 4 TO 6 AS A SIDE DISH

2 cups shelled fresh lima beans

2 cups corn, cut from the cob
    (about 4 ears)

4 tablespoons unsalted butter

1 tablespoon water

1 teaspoon sugar

salt and pepper

¼ cup half-and-half

Place the lima beans, corn, butter, water, sugar, and salt and pepper (to taste) in the slow cooker. Set the slow cooker to low and cook for 2 to 2½ hours, until the vegetables are almost tender. Season to taste, add the half-and-half, and stir to mix. Cook an additional 30 minutes. Serve hot.

Escalloped Eggplant with Tomatoes and Onions

August 1927

SERVES 6 TO 8 AS A SIDE DISH

2 tablespoons olive oil

2 large yellow onions, thinly sliced

butter

2 large purple eggplants, peeled
    and cut into ½-inch slices

4 to 6 large, ripe-but-firm
    beefsteak tomatoes, sliced

salt and pepper

Heat the olive oil in a large skillet and cook the onions until they are translucent and just beginning to turn golden.

    Butter the inside of the slow cooker. Place a layer of eggplant on the bottom, followed by a layer of tomatoes, a coating of onions, a sprinkle of salt and pepper, and dots of butter. Repeat the sequence until all the vegetables are used. Sprinkle on a final bit of salt and pepper and a dotting of butter. Set the slow cooker to low and cook for 2 to 3 hours, until the vegetables are tender but still hold their shape. If the eggplant begins to stick to the bottom of the dish during cooking, you may add 1 tablespoon of water.

Fried Green Tomatoes

September 1928

There are those who long for ripe summer tomatoes, and then there are those who hope for the late-season tomatoes that won't ripen on the vine. Those tomatoes are slightly firm and less juicy, which makes them ideal candidates for breading and frying. If you're feeling particularly hungry, use these fried tomatoes to make the best BLT sandwich you've ever eaten.

SERVES 4 TO 6

4 large, firm, green tomatoes
salt
brown sugar
1 cup dry breadcrumbs or
    cracker crumbs
pan drippings or butter and lard

Slice the green tomatoes into ½-inch slices. Sprinkle the tomatoes with a little salt and a generous amount of brown sugar. Dip the slices in the dry bread or cracker crumbs, patting on as many crumbs as possible.

In a hot skillet, melt some pan drippings or butter and lard. Brown the tomato slices well on one side, then turn and brown on the other. When browned and tender, remove carefully to a serving platter.*

*Note: If you'd like, you can make a dressing out of the pan drippings. In a small bowl, stir together a scant tablespoon of flour in a little cold water. Pour the flour into the pan with the drippings, as well as a cupful of milk. Boil to cook the flour, add salt to taste, and pour around the tomato slices.

Scalloped Tomatoes

April 1910

SERVES 4 TO 6 AS A SIDE DISH

---

1 tablespoon plus 1 teaspoon butter, divided

3 to 4 large beefsteak tomatoes (enough to make 3 layers), ripe but still firm

¾ teaspoon salt

⅓ teaspoon sugar

1 teaspoon minced fresh garlic, divided

freshly ground black pepper

⅓ cup breadcrumbs

2 tablespoons grated Parmesan cheese

Butter the inside of the slow cooker with 1 teaspoon of the butter. Core the tomatoes, cut them in half, and slice into ¼-inch slices. Place them in one slightly overlapping layer at the bottom of the slow cooker and sprinkle with some of the salt and sugar, ½ teaspoon of the garlic, and a little black pepper. Repeat with a second layer, then a third (minus the garlic). Mix the breadcrumbs with the cheese and sprinkle over the top of the tomatoes. Dot with the remaining 1 tablespoon butter and set to cook on low for 2½ hours. Uncover for the last ½ hour of cooking. Serve immediately.

Baked Stuffed Green Peppers

June 1922

SERVES 6

---

6 green bell peppers

2 cups breadcrumbs

2 cups chopped leftover meat

2 eggs, slightly beaten

2 tablespoons butter, melted

milk to moisten

salt and pepper

Cut a round opening in the stem ends of the peppers, remove the seeds and pulp, and soak the peppers in cold water for half an hour. Drain.

Preheat the oven to 375°F. In a large bowl, mix together the breadcrumbs, meat, eggs, butter, enough milk to form a soft, moist mixture, and salt and pepper to taste. Divide the mixture evenly along the peppers. Place the filled peppers in a baking dish and bake at for 40 minutes, or until the peppers are tender. Serve directly from the baking dish or transfer to a platter.

Hot Cabbage Slaw

September 1934

SERVES 4 TO 6 AS A SIDE DISH

1 quart (4 cups) shredded cabbage
¼ teaspoon salt, plus more for
    boiling water
2 tablespoons sugar
1 teaspoon flour
¼ teaspoon powdered mustard
1 egg
½ cup sour cream
¼ cup vinegar

Cook the shredded cabbage for 5 minutes in salted boiling water. Drain the cabbage, put it in a large bowl, and set it aside.

Combine the sugar, flour, powdered mustard, and salt in a small saucepan. Mix in the egg, then stir in the sour cream and vinegar. Bring the mixture to a boil, stirring constantly. Boil for about 2 minutes, then remove the saucepan from the heat and pour the mixture over the cooked cabbage. Before serving, let the cabbage stand in a warm place for a few minutes to absorb the flavor of the sauce. Serve hot.

Potato Pancakes I

May 1918

SERVES 6 TO 8

6 large raw potatoes, grated
1½ teaspoons salt
1 tablespoon milk
1 egg, beaten
3 tablespoons flour
oil or butter, for the pan

In a large bowl, mix together the potatoes, salt, milk, egg, and flour and beat thoroughly. Heat some oil or butter in a large skillet and drop heaping spoonfuls of the potato mixture onto the pan, flipping once to allow each side to brown.

Potato Pancakes II

May 1918

SERVES 2

1 cup boiled potatoes, mashed
    or ground in a ricer
½ teaspoon salt
1 egg, beaten
¼ cup milk
oil or butter, for the pan

In a large bowl, mix together the mashed or riced potatoes, salt, egg, and milk and beat thoroughly. Heat some oil or butter in a large skillet and drop heaping spoonfuls of the potato mixture onto the pan, flipping once to allow each side to brown.

Pea Soufflé

October 1916

Don't let the idea of preparing a soufflé intimidate you. This recipe couldn't be simpler or tastier, as long as you handle your beaten egg whites with care. The key is to maintain the stiff and airy consistency of the egg whites by folding rather than stirring them into the other ingredients. Use a spatula to scoop a dollop of egg whites onto the pea mixture, slide the spatula down the side of the bowl, and fold the pea mixture gently over the egg whites. Repeat this process until all the egg whites have been incorporated into the peas, turning the bowl ¼ turn clockwise with each additional dollop.

SERVES 2 TO 4 AS A SIDE DISH

---

1 cup fresh peas
1 teaspoon salt
pepper
¼ cup milk
4 egg whites

Preheat the oven to 350°F. Grease the bottom and sides of a 1-quart baking dish.

Wash the peas and put them in a small saucepan of water over high heat. Boil the peas until they are tender. Press the peas through a sieve, then add the salt, pepper, and milk.

In a mixing bowl, beat the egg whites until they are stiff and gently fold them into the pea mixture. Transfer to the prepared baking dish and bake for 20 to 30 minutes. Serve the soufflé immediately after removing it from the oven.

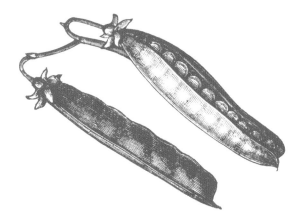

Norwegian Cloob (Potato Dumplings)

February 1928, contributed by Mrs. F.M. D.W., South Dakota

SERVES 8 TO 10

---

12 medium-size potatoes, cooked
    and mashed
12 medium-size potatoes, grated
3 eggs, beaten
1 teaspoon salt
3 tablespoons milk
pork fat, cut into small cubes
3 quarts pork or chicken broth
butter, for serving

Mix together the mashed potatoes, grated potatoes, eggs, salt, and milk. Knead the mixture until it is stiff like bread. Wet your hands with water and knead into balls, placing a small piece of pork fat in the center of each.

In a large pot, bring the pork or chicken broth to a boil, then add the dumplings and simmer for 1 hour. Drain the dumplings and serve with butter.

◆

Oven-Fried Potatoes

May 1934

SERVES 4 (IF 3 MEDIUM RUSSETS ARE USED)

---

3 medium-size potatoes
3 tablespoons butter or bacon fat
salt and pepper

Preheat the oven to 400°F.

Pare the potatoes and cut them lengthwise in strips, as for French fries. Let the potato strips stand in cold water for 15 or 20 minutes while the oven heats.

Melt the butter or bacon fat in a flat, fairly shallow baking dish or a baking sheet. Drain the potatoes thoroughly, stir them in the melted fat until they are coated, and sprinkle them with salt and pepper to taste. Bake for up to 45 minutes, until they are brown, stirring once.

Potato Cheese Sticks

March 1935, contributed by M.R., New York

SERVES 6

---

butter or oil for greasing pan
2 cups warm mashed potatoes
½ cup butter, melted
1 cup grated Cheddar or Jack cheese
1 cup flour
1 teaspoon salt
1 egg yolk
2 tablespoons milk

Preheat the oven to 450°F. Coat the bottom of a baking dish with butter or oil.

In a large bowl, mix the mashed potatoes, butter, cheese, flour, and salt. Cool. Roll into a rectangular sheet ¼ inch thick and cut into strips 4 inches long x ½ inch wide. Carefully transfer the sticks to the prepared baking dish.

In a small bowl, beat the egg yolk and milk together, then brush the mixture onto the sticks. Bake for 10 to 15 minutes. Serve hot with soups and salad. These are less crisp than pastry cheese straws, but very tasty.

Potato Puff

March 1927

SERVES 4 TO 6 AS A SIDE DISH

---

butter or oil for greasing the pan
4 cups hot mashed potatoes
1 tablespoon butter, melted
2 tablespoons milk
1 teaspoon salt
¼ teaspoon pepper
2 eggs, separated

Preheat the oven to 400°F. Grease the bottom of a 2-quart baking dish.

In a large mixing bowl, mix together the mashed potatoes, butter, milk, salt, pepper, and egg yolks. Beat thoroughly. In another bowl, beat the egg whites until stiff, then carefully fold in the stiffly beaten whites into the potato mixture and pile the mixture into the prepared baking dish. Cook for 15 to 20 minutes until the mixture puffs and is brown on the top.

Scalloped Potatoes

November 1922

Scalloped potatoes likely get their name from the Middle English word collop *or the Middle French word* escalope, *both of which mean to slice thinly. As the potato slices cook, the flour dusted over each layer blends with the milk, forming the creamy, satisfying sauce that keeps this dish a perennial favorite. Do your best to slice each potato to the same quarter-inch thickness so the casserole cooks evenly.*

SERVES 6

---

3 pounds potatoes
salt and pepper
¼ cup flour
¼ cup butter
2 cups milk, heated

Preheat the oven to 375°F. Grease the bottom and sides of a 9 x 13-inch baking dish.

Wash, pare, soak, and cut the potatoes in ¼-inch slices. Arrange a layer of potatoes in the bottom of the prepared baking dish, sprinkle them with the salt, pepper, and some of the flour, and dot them with a few pats of the butter. Continue building layers until the potatoes are all in the dish. Add the hot milk to reach the top layer of potatoes. Bake gently until the potatoes are soft and golden.

Bacon-Stuffed Potatoes

September 1929

SERVES 6

6 large potatoes
8 slices bacon, cooked and finely chopped
2 tablespoons butter
salt and pepper

Preheat the oven to 350°F.

Bake the potatoes until they're done, about 1 hour. Remove them from the oven, allow the potatoes to cool for 5 minutes, then roll them slightly. Slice each potato in half lengthwise and scoop out the insides onto a chopping board, reserving the potato shells. Chop the potato flesh into small pieces, place in a large bowl, and add the chopped bacon pieces, butter, and salt and pepper to taste. Mix, then put the filling back into the potato shells. Put the stuffed potatoes in a pan and bake for 10 to 15 minutes, until thoroughly heated through.

Potato au Gratin

September 1929

SERVES 4

2 cups mashed potatoes
3 tablespoons milk
1 teaspoon butter, plus more for topping
salt and pepper
1 cup breadcrumbs
3 tablespoons grated cheese

Preheat the oven to 400°F. Grease the bottom and sides of a round or oval gratin dish or a 1½-quart baking dish.

Beat together the mashed potatoes, milk, butter, and salt and pepper to taste. On the bottom of the prepared dish, thickly strew half the breadcrumbs, spread in the potato mixture, and sprinkle with the cheese. Top with the remaining breadcrumbs, dot with bits of butter, and bake for about 30 minutes.

Camp Fried Potatoes

June 1935

SERVES 6 TO 8 AS A SIDE DISH

2 pounds potatoes
⅓ cup bacon fat or other fat
1 or 2 onions, sliced
salt and pepper

Pare and slice the potatoes into thin strips. Soak the potatoes in cold water until just before you're ready to cook them, then drain thoroughly. Put half the fat in a hot skillet, add half the potatoes and onions, and sprinkle with salt and pepper to taste. Fry the potatoes until they're beginning to brown and get clear. Push the cooked potatoes to one side, add the remaining fat, potatoes, and onions, sprinkle with salt and pepper to taste, and cook until they are all done and nicely browned.

Baked Potato Kugel

September 1929

SERVES 6 AS A SIDE DISH
---

butter for greasing the pan
3 cups grated raw potato
1 medium-size onion, grated
2 tablespoons flour
1 teaspoon baking powder
1 egg, beaten
2 tablespoons melted butter or
    chicken fat
salt

Preheat the oven to 350°F. Grease the bottom and sides of a 9-inch square cake pan.

    Mix the potato, onion, flour, baking powder, egg, butter, and salt to taste, spread in the prepared pan, and bake for about 1 hour or until quite brown.

Scalloped Potatoes with Fresh Pork

September 1929

SERVES 6 TO 8 AS A SIDE DISH

½ pound fresh boneless pork
6 medium-size potatoes, sliced
2 onions, sliced
2 tablespoons flour
salt and pepper
1 tablespoon butter
1 quart (4 cups) milk

Preheat the oven to 350°F.

    Trim the fat from the pork, cut it in small pieces, and put a layer in the bottom of a 9 x 13-inch casserole dish. Put in a layer of sliced potatoes, a layer of onions, and sprinkle with some of the flour and salt and pepper to taste. Dot lightly with some of the butter. Continue to build the layers until you reach within about 2 inches of the top of the dish. End with a layer of pork on top. Sprinkle with salt and pepper and cover all with the milk. Cover the dish and bake for 1 hour. Uncover for the last 10 minutes of baking to brown the meat.

Candied Orange Sweet Potatoes

SERVES 4 TO 6 AS A SIDE DISH
---

butter for greasing the slow cooker
2 large sweet potatoes, peeled and
    sliced ¼-inch thick
1 teaspoon salt
¼ cup unsalted butter, melted
¼ cup brown sugar
½ teaspoon grated orange zest

Butter the inside of the slow cooker and arrange the sweet potatoes inside it in layers, overlapping slightly. Sprinkle with the salt, pour the butter evenly over the potatoes, then sprinkle them with the brown sugar and orange zest. Set the slow cooker to low and cook for 4 hours. Serve immediately.

Sweet Potato Balls

August 1932

*There's not much to **not** love about this tasty little side dish. Creamy, fluffy sweet potatoes? Check. Butter and brown sugar? Check and check. Buttered-breadcrumb coating? Ooooh, yeah. You might as well make an extra batch and serve them for dessert, drizzled in melted chocolate with a side of whipped cream.*

SERVES 4 TO 6 AS A SIDE DISH

---

3 medium-size sweet potatoes
3 tablespoons milk, warmed
2 tablespoons butter
1 tablespoon brown sugar
¼ teaspoon salt
1 egg, beaten
½ cup breadcrumbs

Preheat the oven to 350°F.

In a large saucepan, boil the potatoes with skins on until tender. Peel and mash them in a large bowl. Add the hot milk, butter, brown sugar, and salt. Whip until well mixed and fluffy. Form the potato mixture into small balls, then dip them in the beaten egg, followed by the crumbs. Bake for 15 minutes.

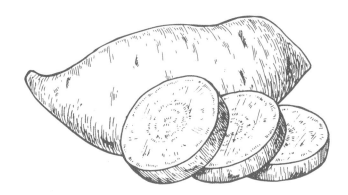

Sweet Potato Puff

November 1924

SERVES 8
---

6 sweet potatoes, peeled and cut
   into cubes
2 tablespoons butter
½ teaspoon salt
2 egg whites, stiffly beaten

Preheat the oven to 400°F. Grease the bottom and sides of eight 8- to 10-ounce custard cups.

  Boil the potatoes until they are soft, transfer them to a large bowl, then mash them together. Add the butter and salt, then fold in the stiffly beaten egg whites. Scoop the potato mixture into the the prepared custard cups. Set the custard cups in a pan of hot water and bake for 20 minutes. Serve hot, straight from the cups.

Stuffed Sweet Potatoes

January 1911

SERVES 6
---

3 large sweet potatoes
1½ tablespoons butter
salt and pepper
heavy cream

Preheat the oven to 400°F.

  Bake the sweet potatoes until they are soft, about 1 hour. When done, cut each potato in half lengthwise and scoop the flesh from the skins. Mash, add ½ tablespoon butter per potato, salt and pepper to taste, and drizzle with heavy cream, beating thoroughly. Refill the emptied skins, set the stuffed potatoes back in the oven, and brown before serving.

Carameled Sweet Potatoes

October 1932

SERVES 8

½ cup butter
1 cup brown sugar
1 (28-ounce) can sweet potatoes

Preheat the oven to 450°F. Melt the butter and sugar together in a baking pan.

  Lay the sweet potatoes, drained, in this syrup. Place the pan in the oven to bake. When the potatoes are browned on the bottom, turn them over so they can brown on the other side.

Sauces

White Sauce

1934

MAKES 1 CUP

---

1 tablespoon butter
1 tablespoon flour
½ teaspoon salt
1 cup milk

To make a thin white sauce, melt the butter in a skillet; add the flour and salt and stir to blend. Add the milk and stir until thickened. This makes a thin white sauce, useful for cream soups and as a sauce for vegetables.

For a medium white sauce, for vegetables, meat, and fish, increase the amount of butter and flour to 2 tablespoons.

For a thick white sauce, for soufflés, increase the butter and flour to 3 tablespoons.

Gravy

MAKES 1 CUP

---

1 tablespoon butter
1 tablespoon flour
1 cup broth
salt and pepper
1 tablespoon pan drippings
  (optional)*

Melt the butter in a skillet; add the flour and stir to blend. Add the broth and stir until thick; season with salt and pepper. This makes a thin gravy.

For thick gravy, use 2 tablespoons drippings and 2 tablespoons flour.

*Note: If you have cooked any sort of meat in a pan or skillet, you can make gravy from the drippings.

Horseradish Sauce

January 1923

MAKES 1½ TO 2 CUPS

¼ cup grated horseradish
½ teaspoon salt
⅛ teaspoon pepper
½ teaspoon powdered mustard
1 teaspoon sugar
1 tablespoon vinegar
1 cup whipping or heavy cream

In a small bowl, combine the horseradish, salt, pepper, mustard, sugar, and vinegar.

In a large bowl, beat the whipping or heavy cream until it forms medium or stiff peaks (as desired). Gently fold the horseradish mixture into the whipped cream to form a thick sauce. Serve with beef.

Mint Sauce

January 1923

MAKES ½ CUP

¼ cup mint leaves, finely chopped
1 tablespoon powdered sugar
½ teaspoon salt
¼ cup vinegar

In a medium-size bowl, combine the mint leaves, powdered sugar, salt, vinegar, and ¼ cup water. Let the sauce stand on the back of the stove for 15 minutes before serving. Serve with lamb.

Currant Sauce

January 1923

MAKES ABOUT 2½ CUPS

½ cup vinegar
½ cup currant jelly
1 cup currants, chopped
1 tablespoon flour

In a medium-size saucepan, boil 1 cup of water. Add the vinegar, currant jelly, and currants and simmer for 10 minutes. Stir the flour with a little cold water to make a smooth paste, then stir it into the sauce to thicken it. Cook thoroughly. Serve with lamb or roast chicken.

Caper Sauce

January 1923

MAKES ABOUT 2½ CUPS (2 TABLESPOONS/SERVING)

½ cup butter
2 tablespoons flour
1½ cups hot water or mutton broth
½ teaspoon salt
½ cup capers, drained

In a medium-size skillet, melt half the butter, stir in the flour, and gradually add the hot liquid, stirring constantly. Add the salt and the remaining butter and capers just before serving. Serve with lamb.

Spiced Cranberries

December 1931

This recipe for a cranberry side dish is almost as easy as opening up a can of the jellied stuff—but it's so much better. The best part is that it won't take up any premium stove space, as it all goes into your slow cooker, where the warm scents of cinnamon and cloves will fill your home for hours. You won't want to keep this gem hidden for holidays only!

SERVES 6 TO 8

---

4 cups cranberries

1½ cups brown sugar

½ cup mild vinegar

1 teaspoon paprika

1 teaspoon ground cinnamon

½ teaspoon ground cloves

½ teaspoon salt

Add the cranberries, brown sugar, vinegar, paprika, cinnamon, cloves, salt, and ¼ cup water to the slow cooker. Stir to combine. Set the slow cooker to low and cook for 2 hours. Raise the temperature to high, remove the cover, and cook an additional ½ to 1 hour to reduce the cooking liquid. Serve hot or cold.

Variation: Stewed Cranberries, a bare-bones holiday dish: Stew 4 cups cranberries with 2 cups sugar and ½ cup water in the slow cooker for 2 to 2½ hours. Remove the cover and cook on high for ½ to 1 hour, if necessary, to reduce the cooking liquid.

Maitre d'Hotel Butter

January 1923

SERVES 4

¼ cup butter
½ teaspoon salt
⅛ teaspoon pepper
½ tablespoon finely chopped parsley
¾ tablespoon lemon juice

Cream the butter and mix in the salt, pepper, and parsley, then add the lemon juice very slowly. Serve with beef.

Honey Butter

August 1933

MAKES SLIGHTLY MORE THAN 1 CUP

---

1 cup granulated or creamed honey
½ cup butter, at room temperature

Blend the honey with the butter. Transfer to a glass jar, screw the cap on the jar, and place it in the refrigerator or someplace where the temperature is 55°F. Honey butter must be kept tightly covered and kept in the refrigerator just as you keep butter.

Serve on toast or pancakes for a delicious breakfast treat.

Buttered Crumbs

February 1932

MAKES 1 CUP

---

1 cup bread pieces
2 tablespoons butter

Spread the bread on a baking sheet and bake at 225°F for 30 to 40 minutes. Roll the dry bread with a rolling pin to crush it into crumbs (or pulverize in a blender or food processor). In a medium-size skillet, melt the butter, add the breadcrumbs, and stir until every crumb is coated.

Desserts

Old-Fashioned Applesauce

October 1938

SERVES 6 TO 8

3 to 4 pounds apples, peeled
    and sliced
¾ cup sugar

Put the apples into a saucepan with ¾ cup water, cover tightly, and cook rapidly without stirring until they begin to boil. The apples should be cooked to a mush by this time. Add the sugar and cook for 2 or 3 minutes longer, stirring constantly. More or less water may be used, depending on how thick you prefer the applesauce to be.

Apple and Peach Sauce

September 1914

SERVES 4

4 apples
2 peaches
¼ cup sugar
cinnamon
cloves, nutmeg, allspice (optional)
cream, for serving

Pare and core the apples, then cut them into quarters. Skin, halve, and remove the pits from the peaches. Put the fruit into a large saucepan with just enough water to prevent burning. Add the sugar, a pinch of cinnamon, and mixed spices to taste, if desired. Cover and cook until the apples are soft and the peaches are tender but not broken. Serve cold with cream, either plain or whipped.

Caramel Raisin Apple 🍚

February 1922

SERVES 6

6 large, firm, tart apples, well washed
½ cup raisins
1 cup light brown sugar
2 tablespoons unsalted butter, plus
    more for greasing the slow
    cooker
½ cup apple juice

Core the apples and peel a bit of the skin from the top. In a small bowl, mix the raisins and sugar together and pack the mixture into the apples. Top each apple with a pat of butter. Butter the slow cooker and arrange the apples inside. Add the apple juice to cover the bottom of the pot. Set the slow cooker to low and cook for 4 to 6 hours until the apples are softened through.

Compote of Apples

October 1912

SERVES 6

---

1 cup sugar

juice of 1 lemon

1 (1-inch) cinnamon stick

6 apples, cored, pared, and cut
in half

whipped cream, for serving

chopped nuts, for serving

Preheat the oven to 350°F.

In a medium-size saucepan, stir together the sugar, lemon juice, and 1 cup of water. Add the cinnamon stick and bring the mixture to a boil. Simmer for 5 minutes, then add the apples and cook them in the syrup until they're almost soft.

Lift the apples from the syrup with a slotted spoon and transfer them to a baking dish. Bake the apples for 10 to 20 minutes, until they are very soft. Continue boiling the syrup until it thickens into a loose jelly.

Remove the apples from the oven and allow them to cool. Fill the apple centers with whipped cream, then pour the thick syrup around the apples; sprinkle with chopped nuts and put whipped cream around the base.

Brown Betty

May 1929

SERVES 6

---

butter for greasing the slow cooker

1 cup breadcrumbs

2 tablespoons butter, melted

1 cup sugar, divided

grated zest and juice of 1 lemon,
divided

1 teaspoon cinnamon

5 sour windfall apples, such as
Granny Smith

heavy cream, for serving

Butter the inside of the slow cooker. In a bowl, mix the breadcrumbs with the melted butter, ½ cup of the sugar, zest, and cinnamon.

Peel and chop the apples into ½-inch cubes. Place the apples in a large bowl and mix with the lemon juice and remaining ½ cup sugar. Spread half of the breadcrumb mixture on the bottom of the slow cooker. Top with the apples and then the remaining breadcrumbs. Set the slow cooker to low and cook covered for 2 hours, then cook uncovered for an additional 30 minutes. Serve hot with a drizzling of heavy cream.

Fruit Cobbler

1934

For those who are averse to making pie crusts, this is the treat for you! But really, who doesn't love a simple summer dessert? Here, all you have to do is put your favorite fruits in the bottom of a pie plate and top it with an easy-to-mix batter. It's a one-bowl recipe, no rolling pin required. Enjoy it fresh from the oven with a large scoop of ice cream.

SERVES 3 ALONE (OR 4 WITH A SCOOP OF ICE CREAM)

butter for greasing the baking dish

1½ cups fresh pitted cherries, chopped apples, cleaned berries, etc.

1 cup flour

⅓ cup sugar

¼ teaspoon salt

1 teaspoon baking powder

¼ cup milk

1 egg, beaten

1 teaspoon butter, melted

Preheat the oven to 400°F. Grease the bottom and sides of an 8- or 9-inch baking dish. Arrange the fruit on the bottom of the baking dish.

In a large bowl, sift together the flour, sugar, salt, and baking powder. Add the milk, egg, and melted butter. Mix and pour over the fruit. Bake the cobbler for 25 minutes, until the top is brown. Serve hot.

Apple Crisp

October 1929

SERVES 6 TO 8

---

butter for greasing the baking dish
4 cups sliced apples (6 to 8 apples)
1 teaspoon cinnamon
1 cup plus 1 teaspoon sugar, divided
¾ cup flour
½ cup butter
1 pint whipped cream, for serving

Preheat the oven to 350°F. Grease the bottom and sides of a 2-quart baking dish.

Cut the apples into ¼-inch slices and place them into the prepared baking dish. Add ½ cup water and the cinnamon.

In a small bowl, mix together 1 cup of the sugar, flour, and butter until crumbly. Spread the topping over the apples and bake uncovered until the apples are soft. Serve hot with the whipped cream, sweetened with the remaining 1 teaspoon sugar.

Deep-Dish Apple Pie

February 1929

SERVES 8

---

6 apples
1 cup sugar
1 egg
½ cup milk
1 tablespoon butter, melted
1 cup flour
pinch of salt
1 teaspoon baking powder

Preheat the oven to 400°F.

Peel and cut the apples into very thin slices. Place the apple slices in a 9-inch deep-dish pie plate* and pour the sugar and 2 tablespoons of water over them. Put them in the oven until they begin to steam.

Meanwhile, in a medium-size bowl, beat the egg and add the milk and butter. Sift together the flour, salt, and baking powder, then stir the flour mixture into the egg mixture.

Reduce the heat to 350°F. Pour the batter over the hot apples and bake until the crust is thoroughly done and a rich brown.

*Note: If possible, a glass dish is preferable, so you can see that both apples and crust are well done.

Poached Pears 🍲

January 1926

SERVES 4

---

2 cups water

1 cup sugar

1 tablespoon grated lemon zest

4 ripe but firm pears, such as Bosc, peeled, cored, and halved

whipped cream, for serving

In a pot on top of the stove, mix together the water, sugar, and lemon zest and boil until it the mixture just begins to thicken into a syrup. Add the syrup to the slow cooker along with the pears and set to low. Cook for 2 to 3 hours until the pears are just tender, stirring occasionally to ensure that the fruit sits in the syrup on all sides. Serve hot with the syrup and sweetened, freshly whipped cream.

Crème de Menthe Pears: Substitute ½ teaspoon mint extract for the lemon zest.

Banana Pudding 🍲

May 1913

SERVES 8

---

butter for greasing the slow cooker

6 small or 4 medium bananas

⅔ cup breadcrumbs

finely grated zest of 2 lemons

4 egg yolks

2 cups milk

1 cup sugar

Butter the inside of the slow cooker.

Peel and mash or purée the bananas until they are smooth. Add them to the slow cooker, followed by the breadcrumbs, lemon zest, yolks, milk, and sugar. Mix well. Set the slow cooker to low and cook for 2 to 3 hours, until set. Serve hot.

Cherry Batter Pudding

June 1927

SERVES 4

---

1 to 1½ pounds cherries, pitted
sugar
1 cup flour
2 teaspoons baking powder
½ cup milk
1 teaspoon unsalted butter, melted
Fruit Sauce (see below)

Preheat the oven to 350°F.

In a large bowl, toss the cherries with a sprinkling of sugar. Pour the cherries into a baking dish, filling no more than three-quarters full.

Sift together the flour and baking powder, then stir in the milk and butter. Beat until the batter is smooth, then spread it over the fruit. Bake until the topping is brown. Serve with the Fruit Sauce.

Fruit Sauce

---

2 cups fruit juice
1 tablespoon cornstarch
3 tablespoons flour
sugar, if needed
pinch of salt
1 teaspoon unsalted butter

Heat the juice in a saucepan. In a small bowl, mix the cornstarch, flour, sugar, and salt, then blend it into the juice. Cook for 10 minutes over medium-low heat, stirring while it thickens. Remove the sauce from the heat and add the butter. Beat thoroughly and serve.

Peach Pudding

September 1912

SERVES 8 TO 10

---

butter for greasing the pan
1 (29-ounce) can peach halves,
    drained
1 cup milk
1 cup sugar
1 egg
2 tablespoons butter, melted
2 teaspoons baking powder
½ cup flour, plus more if needed
cream, for serving

Preheat the oven to 350°F. Grease a 13 x 9-inch baking dish.

Place the canned peach halves in the bottom of the prepared baking dish.

In a medium-size bowl, mix the milk, sugar, egg, butter, baking powder, and flour. If the batter is too thin, add more flour as needed. Drop the batter over the peaches and bake until the batter is nicely browned. Serve with cream.

Coconut Bread Pudding 🍲

September 1923

SERVES 6 TO 8

---

unsalted butter

4 cups stale bread cubes

1 cup shredded unsweetened
    coconut

2 eggs

1½ cups milk

½ cup heavy cream, plus more
    for serving

1 cup sugar

1 tablespoon vanilla extract

ice cream, for serving

Butter the inside of the slow cooker, add the bread and coconut, and mix together. In a large bowl, whisk the eggs, milk, cream, sugar, and vanilla and pour the custard over the bread and coconut. (Note: The custard should thoroughly soak the bread. If it does not, add extra cream and milk until all the bread cubes are moistened.) Set the slow cooker on low and cook for 2½ hours. Remove the lid for the last ½ hour to enhance the crust. Best served warm right out of the slow cooker with a little heavy cream poured over or a small scoop of ice cream.

Cranberry Pudding 🍲

January 1911

SERVES 4 TO 6

---

7 tablespoons unsalted butter, plus
    extra for greasing the slow
    cooker

2 eggs

¾ cup plus 1 tablespoon milk

1 (8-ounce) package (about 2 cups)
    cranberries, fresh or frozen

1½ cups sugar

3 cups flour

2 teaspoons baking powder

heavy cream, for serving

nutmeg, for serving

Grease the inside of the slow cooker.

    Cream together the butter, eggs, and milk in a blender. Put the cranberries in a large bowl, then pour the egg mixture over the berries. Stir in the sugar, and sift in the flour and baking powder. Mix very well and pour into the slow cooker. Set the slow cooker to low and cook for 3 to 4 hours, until just set in the center. Serve with heavy cream and dust with nutmeg.

Variation: In this version of Cranberry Pudding from September 1926, substitute buttermilk for whole milk, and ½ teaspoon baking soda for an equal amount of the baking powder to neutralize the acid in the buttermilk.

Bread Pudding

June 1925

This is a wonderful way to use up leftover bread, which is something nearly every household seems to accumulate in one form or another. Heels from sliced loaves, half a baguette left a day too long in the bag, and even bits of pumpernickel bagel can be stored in a resealable bag in the freezer until enough has accumulated to translate into this classic American dessert. Thaw thoroughly before attempting to cube the bread!

SERVES 4 TO 6

---

2 cups stale bread cubes

1 quart (4 cups) milk, scalded

1 cup sugar

2 eggs, well beaten

½ teaspoon salt

2 tablespoons butter, melted

1 teaspoon vanilla extract
  or ¼ teaspoon cinnamon and nutmeg *or* grated orange or lemon rind

Preheat the oven to 350°F. Grease the bottom and sides of an 8-inch square baking pan.

In a large bowl, soak the bread in the hot milk, cool, and add the sugar, eggs, salt, butter, and desired flavoring (vanilla, cinnamon, or orange or lemon rind). Transfer to the prepared baking pan and bake for 1 hour. Serve with any desired sauce.

Rich Bread Pudding with Meringue: A much finer pudding may be made by using 4 eggs instead of just 2. Put 2 whole eggs and 2 egg yolks in the pudding, then make a meringue of the remaining 2 egg whites. Beat them stiffly with 2 tablespoons of sugar. Spread the meringue over the warm pudding and return the baking dish to the oven until it is well puffed and delicately browned. This is good either hot or cold.

Hominy Pudding

October 1933

SERVES 4

---

butter for greasing the cups
2 cups cooked hominy (grits)
⅔ cup chopped dates or raisins
⅔ cup maple syrup
1 cup milk
1 egg, beaten
¼ teaspoon salt
juice of ½ lemon

Preheat the oven to 350°F. Grease the insides of 4 custard cups.

Thoroughly mix the hominy, dates or raisins, maple syrup, milk, egg, salt, and lemon juice and pour the pudding into the prepared custard cups. Set the cups in a pan of water and bake until set (like a custard).

Caramel Bread Pudding 🍚

December 1911

SERVES 6 TO 8

---

unsalted butter for greasing
    the slow cooker
4 cups stale bread cubes
2 eggs
1½ cups milk
½ cup heavy cream
1 cup brown sugar
1 tablespoon cinnamon

Butter the inside of the slow cooker, then add the bread. In a large bowl, whisk the eggs, milk, cream, brown sugar, and cinnamon, and pour the custard over the bread. (Note: The custard should thoroughly soak the bread. If it does not, add extra cream and milk until all the bread cubes are moistened.) Set the slow cooker on low and cook for 2½ hours. Remove the lid for the last ½ hour to enhance the crust. Serve hot.

Lemon Rice Pudding 🍚

February 1910

SERVES 4

---

unsalted butter for greasing
    the slow cooker
¾ cup basmati rice, rinsed and
    drained
½ cup sugar
1 egg
grated zest of 1 lemon
3 cups milk

Grease the inside of the slow cooker, then add the rice, sugar, egg, lemon zest, and milk. Whisk well, making sure the egg is well beaten-in. Set the slow cooker to low and cook for 2 to 3 hours, until the pudding is a pleasing consistency. Serve hot.

Golden Custard

April 1937, contributed by Mrs. J.A.W., Minnesota

SERVES 6

---

butter for greasing the baking dish
8 egg yolks
⅔ cup sugar
pinch of salt
1½ teaspoons vanilla extract
¼ teaspoon almond extract
3 cups milk
¼ cup cream

Preheat the oven to 325°F. Grease the bottom and sides of a 2-quart baking dish.

In a large bowl, beat the egg yolks; add the sugar. Mix in the salt, vanilla, almond extract, milk, and cream. Pour the custard into the prepared baking dish. Set the baking dish in a pan of hot water. Bake for 50 minutes. Remove the baking dish from the water. Cool and chill.*

Note: This custard is nice served alongside an angel food cake, since both require the same oven temperature (see Pheobe Jane's Angel Food Cake, page 178).

Pineapple Custard

February 1929

SERVES 6

---

5 eggs
½ cup sugar
¼ teaspoon salt
1 quart (4 cups) milk, scalded
1 teaspoon flavoring (such as
     vanilla or pineapple extract)
1½ cups well-drained chopped
     pineapple

In a double boiler, beat the eggs slightly and add the sugar and salt; mix. Very gradually stir in the hot milk, and cook until the mixture coats the spoon. Cool slightly, then stir in the extract of your choice.

Spread the pineapple in a shallow bowl or serving dish, then pour the custard over the pineapple and chill. Serve very cold.

Rice Pudding

February 1927

Cinnamon-scented rice pudding feels like a hug from Grandma and eats like a meal and a dessert all in one when served straight out of the double boiler. A warm early morning pot is a delightful alternative to oatmeal as a special breakfast treat. If you manage to save any for later, store the cooled pudding in the fridge for up to a week. It sets up nicely and tastes just a good cold.

SERVES 4

½ cup uncooked rice

1 cup water

½ cup raisins

stick cinnamon

3 cups milk

½ teaspoon salt

6 tablespoons sugar, plus more
for serving

cinnamon, for serving

cream, for serving (optional)

Combine the rice, water, raisins, and cinnamon in a pan; cover and cook, slowly stirring with a fork when necessary, until the water has been absorbed, about 20 minutes. Add the milk, salt, and sugar and cook for 1 hour in a double boiler. Serve hot with a sprinkling of cinnamon and cream and sugar, if desired.

Chocolate Mousse

December 1931

Mousses can be made in a variety of ways: with whipped cream, eggs (yolks, whites, or both), gelatin, or a combination of these. This frozen version uses an egg to keep large ice crystals from forming during the freezing process—it's what keeps the mousse luscious. If you're at all concerned about eating raw eggs, choose pasteurized eggs.

SERVES 12

---

1 egg
¾ cup powdered sugar
⅛ teaspoon salt
2 tablespoons cocoa paste (made with equal parts unsweetened cocoa powder and cold water, mixed until smooth)
½ teaspoon vanilla extract
1 pint (2 cups) whipped cream

In a medium-size bowl, beat the egg, powdered sugar, salt, cocoa paste, and vanilla thoroughly. Fold the whipped cream into the chocolate mixture.

Prepare a large bowl packed with 1 part salt/1 part ice. Settle the bowl of mousse into the ice bowl, with the ice mixture coming halfway up the side of the mousse bowl. Allow the mousse to sit in a cool place without stirring for 3 to 4 hours before serving.

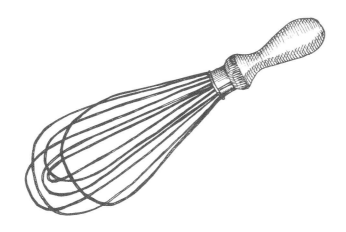

French Vanilla Ice Cream

1934

SERVES 8 TO 10

---

4 egg yolks
⅔ cup sugar
⅛ teaspoon salt
2 cups milk
2 cups cream
½ teaspoon vanilla extract

In a medium-size bowl, combine the egg yolks, sugar, and salt.

Scald the milk in a double boiler and pour slowly, whisking all the while, over the egg yolk mixture. Transfer the mixture back to the double boiler and simmer until the mixture coats a spoon. Chill in the refrigerator, add the cream and vanilla, and freeze in an ice cream maker according to the manufacturer's instructions.

Peanut Brittle Ice Cream: Grind peanut brittle to make 1 cup and add when the ice cream is partially frozen.

Peppermint Ice Cream: Grind peppermint candy to equal 1 cup. Omit the vanilla and decrease the sugar to ½ cup in the foundation recipe. Add the candy when the ice cream is partially frozen.

Sour Cream Chocolate Ice Cream: To the foundation custard recipe add 2 ounces melted bittersweet chocolate and chill. Replace the cream with 1 cup milk and 1 cup sour cream mixed with ⅓ cup sugar.

Baked Alaska

July 1923

SERVES 8

---

6 egg whites
6 tablespoons powdered sugar
1 sponge cake, sliced
1 rectangular, quart-sized carton of ice cream, frozen hard

Preheat the oven to 450°F. Beat the egg whites until stiff and stir in sugar gradually. Wet a wooden board that will fit in your oven on both sides; shake off excess water. Cover the board with parchment, wax, or plain brown paper; lay the sliced cake on top. Cut the ice cream in slices to cover the cake. Spoon meringue on the ice cream and spread it evenly over the top and down the sides. Place the board in the oven and brown the meringue quickly. Slip the dessert from the paper onto a platter and serve at once. This dessert is most appetizing when brought to the table on the platter and served on small plates, giving a portion of cake, ice cream, and meringue with each service.

Cookies and Bars

Jam Marguerites

2 egg whites
3 tablespoons raspberry or
    other jam
2 drops lemon extract
about 20 saltine- or Ritz-type
    crackers
ground nuts

Preheat the oven to 350°F.

Beat the egg whites until they are stiff. Fold in the jam. Add the lemon extract and gently mix. Place by the spoonful on crackers and sprinkle with nuts. Bake until delicately brown, about 10 minutes. Serve strictly fresh.

Black Walnut Crisps: Substitute 6 tablespoons chopped black walnuts for the jam, and vanilla for the lemon extract; add 6 tablespoons sugar.

Marshmallow Marguerites

1 egg white
½ cup marshmallows, cut up
½ cup nuts, chopped
About 20 saltine- or Ritz-type
    crackers

Preheat the oven to 350°F.

Beat the egg white until it is stiff. Fold in the marshmallows and nuts. Mix. Drop small spoonfuls of the mixture on individual crackers and bake until a glaze has formed on top, 8 to 10 minutes. Serve strictly fresh.

Sponge Drops

Adapted from Recipes Tried and True by Cooks

butter for greasing the baking
    sheets
3 eggs
¾ cup sugar
1 cup flour
⅓ teaspoon salt
1 teaspoon baking powder

Preheat the oven to 400°F. Grease your baking sheets.

In a mixing bowl, beat the eggs until they are light, then add the sugar and mix well. Sift in the flour, salt, and baking powder, stir to make a dough, then drop by teaspoonfuls onto the buttered baking sheets. Bake until lightly golden.

Chewy Drop Cookies

MAKES ABOUT 3 DOZEN COOKIES

½ cup unsalted butter, softened,
    plus more for greasing the pans
1 cup sugar
2 egg whites, stiffly beaten
1 teaspoon milk
2 teaspoons baking powder
pinch of salt
1 cup flour

Preheat the oven to 400°F. Grease your baking sheets.

In a mixing bowl, cream the butter and sugar, then add in the egg whites and milk. Sift in the baking powder, salt, and flour and mix well. Drop by teaspoonfuls onto the prepared baking sheets with plenty of room between the cookies. Bake for just a few minutes, watching closely to prevent scorching.

Orange Drop Cookies: To the above, add 1 teaspoon grated orange zest and ⅛ teaspoon baking soda, and substitute 1 teaspoon vanilla extract for the milk.

Brown Sugar Drops

MAKES 1½ TO 2 DOZEN COOKIES

½ cup unsalted butter, plus more for
    greasing pans
¼ teaspoon baking soda
¼ cup buttermilk
1 cup brown sugar, firmly packed
1 large egg
¾ teaspoon baking powder
1½ cups flour
¼ teaspoon salt
1 teaspoon almond extract

Preheat the oven to 325°F. Grease your baking sheets.

In a small bowl, dissolve the baking soda in the buttermilk. Set aside.

In a mixing bowl, cream the brown sugar with the butter; mix in the egg. Sift in the baking powder, flour, and salt, then add the buttermilk mixture and the almond extract. Drop spoonfuls of dough onto the prepared baking sheets and bake 8 to 10 minutes, until lightly browned at edges.

Walnut Cookies

MAKES 4 DOZEN COOKIES

butter for greasing pans
1 teaspoon baking soda
1 cup buttermilk
3 eggs
2 cups sugar
6 cups flour
½ cup walnuts, chopped

Preheat the oven to 350°F. Grease your baking sheets.

In a large bowl, dissolve the baking soda in the buttermilk. Stir in the eggs, sugar, and flour, adding the walnuts last. Roll the dough into balls the size of whole walnuts. Bake until just done, about 15 minutes.

Ginger Drops

Drop cookies are among the easiest treats to bake, so they're a great starter cookie to make with children. Traditional cut out cookies require rolling the dough and using cutters to shape the cookies, but with drop cookies, as their name indicates, your young helpers can simply drop spoonfuls of gooey dough onto the baking sheets. The cookies will take care of the rest since they flatten into circles as they bake.

MAKES 4 TO 5 DOZEN COOKIES

1⅓ cups unsalted butter, softened,
    plus more for greasing the pan

1 cup sugar

4 eggs

2 cups molasses

1 cup sour cream

4 teaspoons baking soda

1 teaspoon cinnamon

2 teaspoons ground ginger

up to 5 cups flour, divided

Preheat the oven to 350°F. Grease your baking sheets.

In a large mixing bowl, cream the butter and sugar, then add the eggs, molasses, and sour cream. Sift in the baking soda, cinnamon, ground ginger, and 1 cup of the flour, stirring to mix together well. Add more flour, ½ cup at a time, until a soft dough forms. Drop spoonfuls of dough onto the prepared baking sheets. Bake until done. Watch closely to prevent burning.

For New Year's Eve Clock Cookies: Make the Ginger Drops as directed, but make the cookies large. Decorate with a clockface made of an icing of powdered sugar and heavy cream mixed together until smooth; apply with a toothpick 12 dashes around the edge of the cookie, and two hands pointed near the hour of 12:00.

Boston Drops

½ cup unsalted butter, softened,
    plus more for greasing the pans
¾ cup sugar
1 egg
1½ cups flour, divided
½ teaspoon baking powder
¼ teaspoon salt
1 teaspoon cinnamon
½ cup chopped raisins
¼ cup walnuts, chopped

Preheat the oven to 400°F. Grease your baking sheets.

In a large mixing bowl, cream the butter and add the sugar slowly, creaming them together. Add the egg, then sift in 1 cup of the flour, baking powder, salt, and cinnamon.

In a small bowl, add the raisins and walnuts, then sift in the remaining ½ cup of the flour and mix together. Add to the batter. Mix thoroughly and drop from a teaspoon 1 inch apart on the prepared baking sheets. Bake for 10 to 15 minutes.

Dutch Drops: Substitute ½ teaspoon lightly crushed aniseed for the cinnamon and ½ cup blanched chopped almonds for the walnuts. Omit the raisins.

English Drops: Add ½ cup cold coffee before adding the flour; increase the sugar to a total of 1 cup and the flour to 1¾ cups. Omit the raisins.

Chocolate Drops

½ cup unsalted butter, softened,
    plus more for greasing the pans
1 egg, well beaten
1 cup brown sugar
2 squares Baker's bittersweet
    chocolate, melted
1½ cups flour, or mix equal parts
    white and wheat flour
¼ teaspoon salt
2 teaspoons baking soda
1½ teaspoons baking powder
½ cup buttermilk
½ teaspoon vanilla extract

Preheat the oven to 350°F. Grease your baking sheets.

In a large mixing bowl, combine the butter, egg, brown sugar, and chocolate. Beat well. Sift in the flour, salt, baking soda, and baking powder. Add the buttermilk and vanilla. Mix thoroughly. Drop from a teaspoon onto the prepared baking sheets about 1 inch apart. Bake for about 15 minutes.

Chocolate Nut Drops: Add ½ cup chopped walnuts to the batter.

Fruit Drops

1 cup unsalted butter, softened,
    plus more for greasing the pans
3 cups brown sugar
¼ cup milk
4 eggs, lightly beaten
2 teaspoons baking soda
5 cups flour, divided
2 cups raisins, chopped
2 cups dried currants
1 cup walnuts, chopped
1 teaspoon cinnamon
4 teaspoons cream of tartar

Preheat the oven to 400°F. Grease your baking sheets.

In a large mixing bowl, cream the butter and brown sugar; add the milk and eggs. Sift the baking soda and half the flour together and add to the mixture. Add the raisins, currants, and walnuts and work well together, then add the cinnamon.

To the remainder of the flour, add the cream of tartar and sift, then add to the dough. Drop by teaspoonfuls onto the prepared baking sheets some distance apart and bake until done.

Sour Cream Drop Cookies

¼ cup unsalted butter, softened,
    plus more for greasing the pans
1¾ cups sugar, divided, plus more
    for dusting
2 eggs, beaten
1 cup sour cream
3 cups flour
½ teaspoon baking soda
1 teaspoon baking powder
½ teaspoon salt
1 tablespoon grated lemon zest
raisins, for garnishing

Preheat the oven to 400°F. Grease your baking sheets.

Cream the butter and ½ cup of the sugar in a large bowl.

In a medium-size bowl, beat the eggs with the remaining 1¼ cups sugar and the sour cream and add to the first mixture.

In a small bowl, sift the flour with the baking soda, baking powder, and salt. Add the lemon zest, then add to the first mixture. Drop small spoonfuls of the dough onto the prepared baking sheets. Top each cookie with 1 raisin and sprinkle with sugar. Bake for 5 to 6 minutes, until very slightly browned at the edges. Be sure not to let these brown all over, since they will dry out quickly in the oven. Remove at once to cooling racks.

Cinnamon Sour Cream Cookies: Add 1 teaspoon vanilla extract and omit the lemon zest and raisins; dust with ¼ cup sugar mixed with 2 teaspoons cinnamon before baking.

Sour Cream Date Cookies: Substitute 2 cups brown sugar for the white sugar, and 1 teaspoon cinnamon and ¼ teaspoon nutmeg for the lemon zest. Add 2 cups chopped dates and 1 cup finely chopped walnuts. Omit the raisins.

Iced Chocolate Drops

MAKES ABOUT 4½ DOZEN COOKIES

½ cup unsalted butter, softened,
    plus more for greasing the pans
1 cup light brown sugar
1 egg
¼ teaspoon baking soda
2 teaspoons baking powder
1½ cups flour
½ cup buttermilk
2 squares bittersweet Baker's
    chocolate, melted
Chocolate Icing (see below)

Preheat the oven to 350°F. Grease your baking sheets.
    In a large mixing bowl, cream the butter and sugar; add the egg and beat well.
    In a small bowl, sift the baking soda and baking powder with the flour and add to the batter alternating with the buttermilk. Add the chocolate. Drop on the prepared baking sheets and bake until done. When cool, spread each cookie with the icing.

Chocolate Icing

1 egg
2 cups powdered sugar
1 teaspoon butter, melted
1 square bittersweet Baker's
    chocolate, melted
cream or milk (optional)

In a large mixing bowl, beat the egg slightly and add the powdered sugar, beating until smooth. Add the butter and chocolate, mix well, and spread on the cookies. If the frosting is a bit stiff, add a touch of cream or milk to make it the right consistency to spread.

Honey Drop Hermits

½ cup unsalted butter, plus more
    for greasing the pans
1⅓ cups honey
1 teaspoon cinnamon
½ teaspoon cloves
½ teaspoon nutmeg
1 egg, beaten
3 to 3½ cups flour
½ teaspoon salt
¾ teaspoon baking soda dissolved
    in ¼ cup water
1 cup chopped raisins or ½ cup
    each nuts and raisins

Preheat the oven to 375°F. Grease your baking sheets.

In a small saucepan, heat the butter and honey together. Add the cinnamon, cloves, and nutmeg to the mixture while it is hot. Cool, then stir in the egg. Transfer the mixture to a large mixing bowl. In a separate mixing bowl, sift together the flour and salt, then add to the butter mixture, alternating with the baking soda in water. Stir in the raisins (and nuts if desired). Beat well. Drop onto the greased pans and bake until just brown.

Peanut Drop Cookies

½ cup unsalted butter, softened,
    plus more for greasing the pans
½ cup smooth peanut butter
1 cup brown sugar
1 egg
½ teaspoon salt
1⅔ cups flour
1 teaspoon baking powder
½ teaspoon baking soda
½ cup milk
1 cup salted peanuts, skinned and
    chopped*

Preheat the oven to 375°F. Grease your baking sheets.

In a large mixing bowl, cream the butter and peanut butter; add the sugar and cream until fluffy. Add the egg and beat thoroughly.

In a small bowl, sift together the salt, flour, baking powder, and baking soda, then add the sifted dry ingredients to the butter mixture, alternating with the milk. Divide the dough in half; to one half add half of the chopped peanuts. Drop by small spoonfuls onto the prepared baking pans, pressing lightly with a finger.

Drop out the other half of the dough in small spoonfuls, stamp down with a glass covered with a damp cloth, and sprinkle with the remaining peanuts.

Bake at 375°F for 8 to 12 minutes.

Walnut Drops: Substitute 1 cup chopped walnuts for the peanuts and add 1 teaspoon vanilla extract.

Hickory Nut Drops: Substitute 1 cup chopped hickory nuts for the peanuts and add 1 teaspoon vanilla extract.

Currant Drops: Substitute 1½ cups currants for the nuts, dredging them in a little flour before adding to the batter; increase the sugar to 1¼ cups and add 1 teaspoon vanilla extract.

*Note: If brown-coated salted nuts are used, put in a salt sack and rub to remove the husks. Fan out the husks by pouring from one pan to another in the wind.

Oatmeal Cookies

MAKES ABOUT 3 DOZEN COOKIES

1½ cups unsalted butter, softened,
    plus more for greasing the pans
1½ cups sugar
2 eggs
2 teaspoons baking powder
1 teaspoon ground cinnamon
2 cups flour
⅓ cup milk or water
2 cups rolled oats

Preheat the oven to 350°F. Grease your baking sheets.
    In a large mixing bowl, cream the butter and sugar, then add the eggs. Sift in the baking powder, cinnamon, and flour, then add the milk or water and, finally, the oats. Mix well and drop onto the prepared baking sheets. Bake until the cookies are browned around the edges.

Ranch Cookies

Adapted from Recipes from Maa Eway

MAKES ABOUT 1½ DOZEN COOKIES

¼ cup unsalted butter, softened
½ cup brown sugar
½ cup granulated sugar
1 egg
½ cup flour
¼ teaspoon baking powder
½ teaspoon baking soda
1 cup rolled oats
½ cup grated unsweetened coconut
½ cup pecans, chopped

Preheat the oven to 350°F. Grease your baking sheets.
    In a large mixing bowl, cream the butter with the brown sugar and granulated sugar, then add the egg. Sift in the flour, baking powder, and baking soda. Mix in the oats, coconut, and pecans. Drop by teaspoonfuls onto the prepared baking sheets. Flatten with your fingers. Bake for 10 to 15 minutes.

Wartime Oatmeal Macaroons

MAKES ABOUT 2 DOZEN MACAROONS

1 tablespoon butter, melted, plus
    more for greasing the pans
1 egg
½ cup corn syrup
2 cups rolled oats
½ teaspoon salt
1 teaspoon baking powder

Preheat the oven to 350°F. Grease your baking sheets.

In a large mixing bowl, add the egg to the melted butter and beat well, then add the corn syrup. Add the oats, salt, and baking powder, and mix. Drop by spoonfuls onto the prepared baking sheets and bake for about 15 minutes.

Coconut Flake Macaroons

April 1931

MAKES ABOUT 3 DOZEN MACAROONS

2 egg whites
1 cup sugar
1 teaspoon vanilla extract
1 cup shredded coconut
1 tablespoon flour
½ cup chopped nuts
2 cups crisp cornflakes

Preheat the oven to 350°F. Grease your baking sheets.

In a large bowl, beat the eggs until stiff peaks form. Add the sugar and vanilla. Fold in the coconut, flour, nuts, and cornflakes. Drop by spoonfuls onto the prepared pans. Bake until lightly golden.

Oatmeal Macaroons

MAKES ABOUT 1 DOZEN MACAROONS

1 tablespoon butter, melted, plus
    more for greasing the pan
¼ cup rolled oats
1 egg
2 tablespoons cream
2 tablespoons milk
1 cup powdered sugar
pinch of cinnamon
2 teaspoons baking powder
1¼ cups flour

Preheat the oven to 350°F. Grease your baking sheet.

In a large bowl, combine the oats, egg, cream, milk, and 2 tablespoons of water. Let it stand until the oats have soaked up all the moisture, then add the powdered sugar, melted butter, and cinnamon.

In a small bowl, sift together the baking powder and flour and add it to the mixture. Drop the dough onto the prepared baking sheet by spoonfuls as large as walnuts and bake for 10 minutes.

Almond Macaroons

These delicate little cookies are the perfect accompaniment for afternoon tea—or anytime you simply want a sweet treat. They're quite simple to make, so try a few batches with the variations (below) to serve all at once. While the cream of tartar is optional, it will help stabilize your egg whites as well as improve their volume (so you'll have a lighter cookie).

MAKES 1 TO 2 DOZEN MACAROONS

2 egg whites

⅛ teaspoon cream of tartar (optional)

1½ cups powdered sugar, sifted

½ cup almond flour, pressed through a sieve if grind is not very fine

Preheat the oven to 325°F. Line baking sheets with parchment paper.

Beat the egg whites until very stiff, adding the cream of tartar if desired. Very gradually incorporate the powdered sugar until the mixture is thick and gluey. Fold in the almond flour and drop (or pipe) onto the prepared baking sheets. Bake for 10 to 15 minutes, until just set—do not allow to brown. Remove immediately from the paper.

Hickory Nut Macaroons: Substitute 1 cup hickory nuts, ground fine in a food processor and then sieved, for almond flour.

Pistachio Macaroons: Substitute 1 cup pistachio nuts, ground fine in a food processor and then sieved, for almond flour.

Coconut Macaroons: Substitute 1 cup coconut, ground fine in a food processor and then sieved, for almond flour.

Fruit Macaroons: Sprinkle up to ½ cup currants or very finely chopped dates or raisins over the batter just before spooning onto the baking sheets.

Chocolate Macaroons: To the beaten egg whites, fold in 2 slightly beaten egg yolks. Mix the almond flour with ½ cup grated semisweet chocolate (or run ½ cup chocolate chips through the blender, until pulverized) and a few drops of vanilla extract. Bake for 12 to 15 minutes. This will result in a delicate version of a chocolate chip cookie. *Alternately*: Melt ½ cup semisweet chocolate and allow to cool completely. Mix into the egg yolks and fold into the beaten egg whites.

Simplest Meringue

2 egg whites
½ cup powdered sugar
½ teaspoon vanilla extract

Preheat the oven to 225°F. Line baking sheets with parchment paper.

Beat the egg whites until stiff. Fold in the sugar and the vanilla. Drop in small shapes onto the prepared baking sheets. Bake very slowly (dry rather than bake) for half an hour or longer.

Coconut Meringues: Sprinkle with desiccated coconut before baking.

Chocolate Meringues: Add 2 teaspoons cocoa powder with the sugar.

Nut Meringues: Finely chopped nuts may be sprinkled over the meringues before baking.

Candied Meringues: Tiny candies, such as sugared caraway seeds, may be put on top before baking.

Meringue Sandwich Cookies: After baking, 2 meringues may be put together, back to back, with any frosting (or jam).

Chocolate Ice Box Cookies

Kansas

MAKES ABOUT 2 DOZEN COOKIES

½ cup unsalted butter, softened plus more for greasing the pans
1 cup sugar
1 egg, beaten
2 squares bittersweet Baker's chocolate, melted
2 cups flour
¼ teaspoon salt
2 teaspoons baking powder
¼ cup milk

In a large mixing bowl, cream the butter, add the sugar, and blend well. Add the egg and chocolate and continue to beat.

In a small bowl, sift together the flour, salt, and baking powder, then add the sifted dry ingredients to the butter mixture alternating with the milk. Chill the dough, and when firm, roll out and shape into logs the size of a tumbler. Chill again until firm.

Preheat the oven to 350°F. Grease your baking sheets. Cut the chilled logs into thin slices. Bake for about 10 minutes.

Note: The dough may be kept in refrigerator for several days, wrapped in waxed paper.

Apricot Oatmeal Cookies

1 cup unsalted butter, softened, plus more for greasing the pans

¾ cup granulated sugar

1 cup brown sugar, tightly packed

2 eggs

1 teaspoon vanilla extract

1½ cups flour

1 teaspoon salt

1 teaspoon baking soda

3½ cups rolled oats

1½ cups dried apricots, finely chopped

1 cup pecans, chopped

In a large mixing bowl, cream the butter, granulated sugar, and brown sugar; add the eggs and vanilla and mix well. Sift in the flour, salt, and baking soda. Add the oats, apricots, and pecans and mix well. Shape into logs and wrap in waxed paper. Refrigerate overnight.

Preheat the oven to 350°F. Grease your baking sheets. Cut the chilled dough into ½-inch-thick slices and place on the prepared baking sheets. Bake for 10 to 15 minutes, until lightly browned.

Soft Sugar Cookies

September 1931

½ cup unsalted butter, softened, plus more for greasing the pans

1 cup sugar plus more for dusting

2 eggs, well beaten

grated zest of 1 lemon

1 tablespoon milk

2¼ cups flour

2 teaspoons baking powder

½ teaspoon nutmeg

Preheat the oven to 425°F. Grease your baking sheets.

In a large bowl, cream the butter thoroughly, add the sugar gradually, and cream together until light and fluffy. Add the eggs, lemon zest, and milk and beat well. Sift in the flour, baking powder, and nutmeg a small amount at a time. Beat after each addition until smooth.

Roll into a thin sheet on a slightly floured board. Cut with floured cookie cutters, place on the prepared baking sheets, and dust with sugar. Bake until delicate brown.

Vanilla Cookies

The key to soft sugar cookies, as any grandmother knows, is to pull them from the oven before they're too brown. Allow them to set on the baking sheet for just 1 minute before removing to a cooling rack.

MAKES 3 TO 4 DOZEN COOKIES

1½ cups sugar, plus more for
    dusting (optional)
½ cup unsalted butter, softened,
    plus more for greasing the pans
1 teaspoon vanilla extract
2 egg yolks
½ cup sour cream
1 tablespoon milk
3¾ cups flour
½ teaspoon salt
½ teaspoon baking soda

In a large mixing bowl, cream the sugar and butter, then add the vanilla and egg yolks. Mix in the sour cream and milk, then sift in the flour, salt, and baking soda. Mix well to make a stiff dough. Cover and refrigerate for 1 hour.

Preheat the oven to 375°F. Grease your baking sheets. Roll out the chilled dough very thin on a floured board and cut into shapes with cookie cutters. Place the cutouts on the prepared baking sheets, dust with sugar if desired, and bake for about 10 minutes.

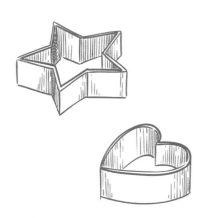

Rolled Fruit Cookies

1 cup unsalted butter, softened,
    plus more for greasing the pans
2 cups sugar
3 eggs, slightly beaten
1 teaspoon cinnamon
1 teaspoon ground cloves
⅓ teaspoon baking soda
2 teaspoons baking powder
up to 3 cups flour, divided
3 tablespoons cold coffee or
    fruit juice
1 cup raisins, chopped and
    dredged in a little flour

Preheat the oven to 350°F. Grease your baking sheets.

In a large mixing bowl, cream the butter and sugar. Add the eggs and beat until light. Sift in the cinnamon, cloves, baking soda, baking powder, and ½ cup of the flour and beat well. Add the coffee, then the raisins. Beat all together, then add the remaining 2½ cups flour, ½ cup at a time, to make a soft dough.

Roll out on a floured board and use cookie cutters to cut into shapes. Place the cutouts on the prepared baking sheets and bake for 15 to 20 minutes.

Orange Butter Thins

Adapted from The Pennsylvania Dutch Cook Book

2 cups unsalted butter, softened,
    plus more for greasing the pans
1 teaspoon baking soda
½ cup sour cream
3½ cups powdered sugar
5 eggs
4 cups flour
¼ teaspoon salt
1 teaspoon orange extract

Preheat the oven to 350°F. Grease your baking sheets.

In a small bowl, dissolve the baking soda in the sour cream. Set aside.

In a large mixing bowl, cream the butter and sugar, then add the eggs. Sift in the flour and salt, then add the sour cream mixture and the orange extract.

Roll out very thin on a floured board. Cut with cookies cutters and place the cutouts on the prepared baking sheets. Bake for about 10 minutes.

Ginger Creams

1 cup unsalted butter, plus more
    for greasing the pans
2 cups molasses
1 tablespoon powdered ginger
1 tablespoon baking soda
4 to 6 cups flour
Frosting (see below)

Preheat the oven to 350°F. Grease your baking sheets.

In a large mixing bowl, beat together the butter, molasses, ginger, baking soda, and flour, using just enough flour that the dough doesn't become too stiff.

Roll out thick on a floured board and cut with a small (2-inch) cookie cutter. Place the cutouts on the prepared baking sheets and bake for 6 to 10 minutes, until the cookies are just beginning to brown around the edges. Take care not to scorch. Allow the cookies to cool for a few minutes before removing to a cooling rack. Spread the frosting on the cookies when they are cool.

Orange Ginger Creams: Add 1 tablespoon grated orange zest.

Spicy Ginger Creams: Add 1 teaspoon black pepper.

Frosting

1 cup sugar
3 tablespoons hot water
2 egg whites, beaten

In a small saucepan, heat the sugar and water, stirring until they hair (230°F to 234°F on a candy thermometer). Then slowly pour the sugar mixture into the egg whites, beating all the while until cool. Spread on the cookies.

Oatmeal Snap Cakes

½ cup fine oatmeal
2 cups flour
pinch of salt
2 tablespoons sugar
2 teaspoons baking powder
1 egg
½ cup heavy cream
½ cup milk

Preheat the oven to 350°F.

In a large mixing bowl, stir together the oatmeal, flour, salt, sugar, and baking powder.

In a small bowl, beat the egg until light, then add the cream and milk and stir together. Add the egg mixture to the oatmeal mixture, using a fork to combine the ingredients into a light dough.

Roll the dough out on a floured board until thin, cut into circles, and transfer to a baking sheet. Bake until done.

Rich Peanut Butter Cookies

November 1934

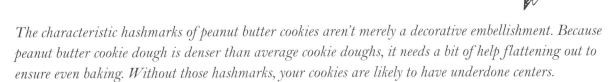

The characteristic hashmarks of peanut butter cookies aren't merely a decorative embellishment. Because peanut butter cookie dough is denser than average cookie doughs, it needs a bit of help flattening out to ensure even baking. Without those hashmarks, your cookies are likely to have underdone centers.

MAKES 4 DOZEN COOKIES

½ cup lard
½ cup butter
1 cup granulated sugar
1 cup brown sugar
1 cup peanut butter
2 eggs, beaten
1 teaspoon vanilla extract
3 cups flour
1 teaspoon baking soda
½ teaspoon salt

Preheat the oven to 375°F.

In a large mixing bowl, cream the lard, butter, granulated sugar, and brown sugar. Add the peanut butter and mix well. Add the eggs and vanilla extract and beat well.

In a small bowl, sift together the flour, baking soda, and salt, then add to the peanut butter batter. Mix well. Use your hands to shape the dough into balls. Place each ball about 2 inches apart on baking sheets and press with a fork to flatten and mark with a cross. Bake until delicately browned.

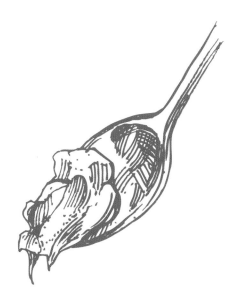

Snickerdoodles

Adapted from Hot Recipes

MAKES 4 TO 5 DOZEN COOKIES

---

1 cup unsalted butter, softened,
    plus more for greasing the pans
1½ cups sugar, divided
1 tablespoon cinnamon
2 eggs
2¾ cups flour
1 teaspoon baking soda
2 teaspoons cream of tartar
½ teaspoon salt
¼ teaspoon nutmeg
1 cup walnuts, finely chopped
1 cup raisins, finely chopped

Preheat the oven to 400°F. Grease your baking sheets.

In a small bowl, combine ½ cup of the sugar with the cinnamon. Set aside.

In a large mixing bowl, cream the butter and the remaining 1 cup sugar, then add the eggs. Sift in the flour, baking soda, cream of tartar, salt, and nutmeg then mix in the nuts and raisins. Form the dough into small balls, place on the prepared baking sheets, and flatten; dust with the cinnamon and sugar. Bake for 8 to 10 minutes.

Cinnamon Shortbread

Adapted from The Meetinghouse Cookbook

MAKES ABOUT 2 DOZEN COOKIES

---

1 cup unsalted butter, softened,
    plus more for greasing the pans
1 cup sugar, divided
1 tablespoon cinnamon
½ cup sugar
3 cups flour
¼ teaspoon nutmeg
3 egg yolks
1 egg white, lightly beaten

Preheat the oven to 375°F. Grease your baking sheets.

In a small bowl, combine ½ cup of the sugar with the cinnamon. Set aside.

In a large mixing bowl, cream the butter and the remaining ½ cup sugar. Sift in the flour and nutmeg and mix until smooth, then add the egg yolks.

Roll the dough thin on a floured board and cut the dough with cookies cutters. Place the cutouts on the prepared baking sheets, brush with the egg white, and sprinkle with the cinnamon and sugar. Bake for 12 to 15 minutes until lightly browned around the edges.

Scotch Shortbread

April 1923

MAKES 3 TO 4 DOZEN COOKIES

---

3 cups flour
2 cups butter
1 cup sugar
1 ounce blanched almonds

Preheat the oven to 300°F.

Sift the flour twice and rub in the butter with your hands. Add the sugar and knead and mix either on a board or in a bowl until a dough is formed. Do not add either egg or milk, as the butter softens the mixing and will bind the ingredients together. Roll the dough rather thinly, cut into rounds or ovals, and press a few almonds onto each. Bake in a pie pan until golden brown.

Sour Cream Molasses Cookies

MAKES ABOUT 4 DOZEN COOKIES

---

1 cup unsalted butter, plus more
    for greasing the pan
1 cup brown sugar
1 cup molasses
3 eggs, beaten
1 cup sour cream
2 teaspoons baking soda
1½ teaspoons salt
1½ teaspoons ground ginger
1 tablespoon cinnamon
up to 6 cups flour, divided
Cookie Icing (optional, see recipe
    below)

In a large mixing bowl, cream the butter with the sugar, then add the molasses, eggs, and sour cream.

In a small bowl, sift the baking soda together with the salt, ginger, cinnamon, and 1 cup of the flour and mix into the dough. Add just enough flour, 1 cup at a time, to make a soft batter. Chill the dough for several hours.

Preheat the oven to 350°F. Grease your baking sheets. Roll out the chilled dough on a floured board and cut the dough into shapes with cookie cutters. Place the cutouts on the prepared baking sheets and bake for 12 to 15 minutes. When cool, spread with Cookie Icing, if desired.

Sour Cream Molasses Bars: Spread the batter without chilling in a greased 9 x 13-inch pan and bake at 350°F. While still warm, dust with powdered sugar. Cut into bars when ready to serve.

Cookie Icing

½ cup sugar
1½ tablespoons water
1 tablespoon unsalted butter
few drops vanilla extract

Boil together the sugar, water, and butter to the soft-ball stage (234°F to 240°F registered on a candy thermometer). Whisk until cool and creamy, then add the vanilla and spread on the cookies.

Filled Cookies

1 cup sour cream
2 cups sugar
3 cups flour
½ teaspoon baking soda
½ teaspoon salt
1 teaspoon vanilla extract
jam, or the filling of your choice
(see below)

Preheat the oven to 400°F.

In a large mixing bowl, blend the sour cream and sugar; sift in the flour, baking soda, and salt, then add the vanilla. Place a portion of the dough on a well-floured board and roll thin. Cut to the desired size with a cutter that has been dipped in flour. Do not put the floured scraps together after making the cutouts; the flour that adheres to the scraps will make a stiffer dough and a less tender cookie.

After the cookies have been cut, put a small amount of cooked filling in the center of one cookie and place another cookie on top of it. Press the edges together and bake until nicely golden.

Raisin Filling

1 cup raisins, chopped
½ cup sugar
½ cup water
1 teaspoon flour

Combine the raisins, sugar, water, and flour in a double boiler and cook until thick. Cool before spreading.

Fig Filling

1½ cups dried figs, chopped
½ cup water
⅓ cup sugar

Mix the figs, water, and sugar in a double boiler and cook until thick. Cool before spreading.

Date Filling

1½ cups dates
⅓ cup sugar
¼ cup water

Wash the dates and remove any pits. Add to a double boiler along with the sugar and water and cook until thick. Cool before spreading.

Apricot Filling

1 cup dried apricots, chopped
¼ to ⅓ cup sugar, depending on
    your preference
¾ cup water

Place the apricots, sugar, and water in a saucepan and cook over low heat until thick and smooth, adding more water if necessary. Cool before spreading.

Apple Filling

1 cup chopped apples
1 tablespoon chopped preserved
    ginger
½ cup sugar
juice and grated zest of 1 orange
½ cup nuts, chopped

In a saucepan, mix together the apples, ginger, sugar, orange juice, orange zest, and nuts. Cook until thick and the apples are clear. Cool before spreading.

Spiced Oatmeal Cookies

1934

butter for greasing the pans
2 teaspoons cinnamon
1 teaspoon nutmeg
1 teaspoon ground allspice or cloves
1 cup shortening
2 cups brown sugar
2 eggs
1 cup buttermilk*
2½ cups flour
1 teaspoon baking soda
¾ teaspoon salt
2 cups rolled oats
2 cups raisins
1 cup chopped nuts (optional)

Preheat the oven to 350°F. Grease your baking sheets.

In a small bowl, mix together the cinnamon, nutmeg, and allspice or cloves. Set aside.

In a large bowl, cream the shortening with the brown sugar.

In a small bowl, beat the eggs and mix in the buttermilk.

In another small bowl, mix the flour well with the baking soda, salt, and 1 tablespoon of the spice mixture. Stir in the rolled oats, raisins, and nuts (if using).

Alternate adding the liquid and dry ingredients to the creamed shortening and sugar. Drop spoonfuls onto the prepared pans and bake for about 15 minutes.

Bran Cookie: Substitute bran for the oats for a bran drop cookie.

*Note: If you don't have buttermilk, use a scant cup of milk; decrease the baking soda to ½ teaspoon; add 2 teaspoons baking powder.

Sandbakkels

MAKES 3 TO 4 DOZEN COOKIES

1 pound unsalted butter, softened, plus more for greasing the forms
1⅛ cups sugar
1 egg
4 cups flour
½ teaspoon salt
1 cup almond flour

Preheat the oven to 350°F. Grease the insides of the sandbakkel cookie forms (traditionally, small, fluted, metal tart-like tins).

In a large bowl, cream the butter and sugar, then add the egg. Stir in the flour, salt, and almond flour. Press small bits into the cookie forms and place them on baking sheets. Bake until delicately browned. Cool slightly and invert to remove the cookies from the forms.

Norwegian Krumkake

Contributed by Mrs. W.J., Minnesota

MAKES ABOUT 4 DOZEN KRUMKAKE

1 cup unsalted butter, melted
1¾ cups sugar
2 cups flour
6 eggs
1 teaspoon vanilla extract

Combine the butter, sugar, flour, eggs, vanilla, and 1 cup cold water. Mix well to remove any lumps. Bake on a krumkake iron until golden. Remove and roll into a cone shape right away, while the cookie is still warm and rollable.

Note: This recipe requires a krumkake iron, a contraption resembling a waffle iron that sits atop a stove burner and embosses a slight design on the cookie as it "bakes." The cookie is then rolled into a cone shape while warm.

Swedish Spritz Cookies

Contributed by Mrs. A.J., Iowa

MAKES 4 DOZEN COOKIES

1 cup unsalted butter, softened
1 cup sugar
1 egg
2 teaspoons almond extract
2½ to 3 cups flour (enough to make a stiff dough)

Preheat the oven to 400°F.

In a large mixing bowl, cream the butter and sugar, then add the egg, almond extract, and just enough of the flour to make a stiff dough. Force the dough through a cookie press to form into rings or fancy shapes. Place the cookies on unbuttered baking sheets and bake, taking care not to burn.

Date Butterballs

½ cup unsalted butter, softened
⅓ cup powdered sugar, plus more
    for rolling
1 tablespoon milk
1 teaspoon vanilla extract
1 ¼ cups flour
¼ teaspoon salt
1 cup dates, pitted and finely
    chopped
½ cup walnuts, finely chopped

Preheat the oven to 350°F.

In a large mixing bowl, cream the butter and sugar. Mix in the milk and vanilla, then sift in the flour and salt. Finally, stir in the dates and nuts and mix well. Form the dough into 1-inch balls and place on unbuttered baking sheets. Bake for about 20 minutes, until lightly browned. Remove from the sheets and roll in powdered sugar while they're still warm, then again before serving.

Almond Butterballs

1 cup unsalted butter, softened
¼ cup powdered sugar
1 teaspoon almond extract
2 cups flour
1 cup blanched almonds, chopped

Preheat the oven to 350°F.

In a large mixing bowl, cream the butter and sugar, add the extract, then sift in the flour. Mix in the almonds. Form the dough into 1-inch balls and place them on unbuttered baking sheets. Bake for about 20 minutes.

Molasses Butterballs

These two-bite cookies are a fine addition to a holiday tray with the warm notes of molasses and earthy walnuts. When rolled in confectioners' sugar, they make such pretty little snowballs. To ensure the powdered sugar fully coats, roll them once when they come out of the oven and again when they've fully cooled.

MAKES ABOUT 4 DOZEN COOKIES

1 cup unsalted butter, softened
¼ cup molasses
2 cups flour
½ teaspoon salt
2 cups walnuts, chopped
powdered sugar, for rolling

Preheat the oven to 350°F.

In a large mixing bowl, cream the butter, then add the molasses and mix well. Sift in the flour and salt, then mix in the nuts. Form the dough into 1-inch balls and place them on unbuttered baking sheets. Bake for about 25 minutes, until lightly browned. Remove from the sheets and roll in powdered sugar while they're still warm, then again before serving.

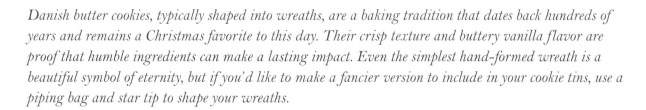

Danish Love Krandse

March 1927, contributed by Miss S.R., Nebraska

Danish butter cookies, typically shaped into wreaths, are a baking tradition that dates back hundreds of years and remains a Christmas favorite to this day. Their crisp texture and buttery vanilla flavor are proof that humble ingredients can make a lasting impact. Even the simplest hand-formed wreath is a beautiful symbol of eternity, but if you'd like to make a fancier version to include in your cookie tins, use a piping bag and star tip to shape your wreaths.

MAKES 4 TO 5 DOZEN COOKIES

---

4 hard-cooked egg yolks

1 cup butter

½ cup sugar, plus extra for dipping

3 cups flour

1 teaspoon vanilla extract

1 egg, lightly beaten

Rub the egg yolks through a sieve. In a bowl, cream the butter and sugar, and mix with the flour. Add the egg yolks and vanilla. Roll the dough into thin ropes, 4 to 5 inches long, and form into wreaths. For a fancier presentation, use a star tip to pipe a wreath shape. Dip the cookies in the beaten egg and sugar. Place on baking sheets and bake.

Ice Box Cookies

1934

MAKES 3 TO 4 DOZEN COOKIES

---

1 cup butter or part other fat
½ cup lard
1 cup granulated sugar
1 cup brown sugar, firmly packed
3 eggs, slightly beaten
½ teaspoon salt
1 teaspoon cinnamon
½ teaspoon baking soda
1 teaspoon baking powder
4½ cups flour, divided
1 cup nut meats

In a large mixing bowl, cream the butter, lard, granulated sugar, and brown sugar. Add the eggs and beat well.

In a small bowl, sift the salt, cinnamon, baking soda, and baking powder with 1 cup of the flour; add to the first mixture and beat well.

Mix the nut meats with the remaining 3½ cups flour and add it to the dough. Mold the dough into 2 well-shaped loaves and chill in the refrigerator overnight.

In the morning, preheat the oven to 450°F. Slice the loaves into cookies and bake until the edges are golden.

Viennese Almond Cookies

December 1936

MAKES ABOUT 3 DOZEN COOKIES

½ cup butter
1¾ cups sifted flour
½ cup sugar, plus more for rolling
½ cup finely ground, blanched
  almonds plus more for rolling
2 egg yolks, beaten
2 to 2½ tablespoons cream
Chocolate Icing (see page 142,
  optional)

Preheat the oven to 350°F.

In a large bowl, work the butter into the flour until it is mealy (finer than for pie crust). Add the sugar and nuts and mix well. Add the beaten yolks, followed by the cream. The dough should be soft enough to handle without breaking.

For "horseshoes," roll into long strips about the thickness of a pencil. Cut into 3-inch lengths and shape each piece as a crescent or horseshoe. Bake for 15 minutes. While warm, roll in a mixture of sugar and ground nuts. Cover the ends with a thin chocolate icing, if desired.

Jelly Circles: Roll out the dough quite thick, about ½ inch. Cut out very small rounds with a tiny cutter or wineglass. Make a dent in the center and put in a fleck of bright jelly. Sprinkle with ground nuts and sugar around the edge. Bake for 10 to 15 minutes at 400°F.

German Springerle

February 1928, contributed by Mrs. A.W., Illinois

MAKES ABOUT 1 DOZEN COOKIES

---

7 eggs, separated
3 cups powdered sugar
1 teaspoon grated nutmeg
1 teaspoon cinnamon
1 teaspoon vanilla extract
1 square unsweetened chocolate, grated
2 tablespoons butter, slightly softened
1 teaspoon baking powder
1 cup flour, divided

In a large bowl, beat the egg whites until stiff. Set aside.

In a large mixing bowl, beat the egg yolks, sugar, nutmeg, cinnamon, vanilla, chocolate, and butter. Fold in the beaten egg whites. Mix the baking powder with ½ cup of the flour and stir or knead into the mixture. Turn out onto a well-floured board and knead in as much of the remaining ½ cup flour as the dough will hold. Roll very thin and mold over a single springerle mold or mold of any kind. Press the dough on the mold to make the design distinct. Cut the cakes out and lay them on the table. Cover with a clean cloth and let dry overnight.

In the morning, preheat the oven to 350°F. Bake for about 20 minutes.

Chocolatey Fruit & Nut Squares

MAKES 16 BARS

---

1 cup unsalted butter, melted, plus more for greasing the pan
1 cup dates, finely chopped
1 cup boiling water
1 teaspoon baking soda
1 teaspoon salt
1 teaspoon vanilla extract
1 cup sugar
2 eggs
1⅓ cups flour
12 ounces semisweet chocolate chips
¼ cup walnuts, chopped

Preheat the oven to 350°F. Grease the bottom and sides of a 9-inch square baking pan.

In a large bowl, mix the butter, dates, boiling water, baking soda, salt, vanilla, sugar, eggs, and flour. Spread in the prepared baking pan. Cover with the chocolate chips and nuts and bake for 40 minutes. Cool. Cut into bars to serve.

Apple Blondies

Adapted from Favorite Recipes of the King's Daughters and Sons

Think of these snackable bars as upgraded apple-walnut muffins. They have the rich gooeyness of blondies with the warming fall scent of cinnamon and nutmeg. Easy to mix in one bowl, they're quick enough for after school, but they're just special enough for company.

SERVES 9

½ cup unsalted butter, softened,
    plus more for greasing the pan

¾ cup sugar

1 egg

1 cup flour

½ teaspoon baking powder

½ teaspoon baking soda

1 teaspoon cinnamon

⅛ teaspoon nutmeg

1 cup cored, peeled, and
    finely chopped apples

1 cup walnuts or almonds, finely
    chopped

Preheat the oven to 350°F. Grease the bottom and sides of an 8-inch square baking pan.

In a large bowl, cream the butter and sugar, add the egg, then sift in the flour, baking powder, baking soda, cinnamon, and nutmeg. Mix in the apples and nuts and pour the batter into the prepared baking pan. Bake for 30 to 35 minutes. Cool and cut into squares to serve.

Brownies

MAKES 16 BROWNIES

¼ cup unsalted butter, melted,
 plus more for greasing the pan
1 cup sugar
1 egg
2 ounces bittersweet Baker's
 chocolate, melted
¾ teaspoon vanilla extract
½ cup flour
½ cup chopped walnuts (optional)

Preheat the oven to 350°F. Grease the bottom and sides of an 8- or 9-inch square baking pan.

In a large bowl, mix together the butter, sugar, egg, chocolate, vanilla, and flour. Add the nuts, if using. Spread the batter evenly in the prepared baking pan. Bake for 25 to 30 minutes. Turn out the brownies and cut into squares to serve.

Blondies

MAKES 16 BLONDIES

⅔ cup unsalted butter, softened,
 plus more for greasing the pan
⅔ cup brown sugar
4 eggs
⅔ cup molasses
2 cups flour
2 cups walnuts, finely chopped

Preheat the oven to 350°F. Grease the bottom and sides of an 8- or 9-inch square baking pan.

In a large mixing bowl, cream the butter and brown sugar, add the eggs and molasses, then the flour and the nuts. Pour the batter evenly into the prepared baking pan and bake for 15 to 20 minutes. Cut into squares to serve.

Cocoa Sticks

Contributed by H.R., Wisconsin

MAKES ABOUT 1 DOZEN STICKS

½ cup unsalted butter, softened
1 cup sugar
2 eggs
1 cup flour
3 tablespoons unsweetened cocoa
 powder
2 tablespoons milk
1 teaspoon vanilla extract

Preheat the oven to 400°F. Grease the bottom and sides of a 13 x 9-inch baking pan.

In a large bowl, cream the butter and sugar, then add the eggs.

In a small bowl, sift together the flour and cocoa. Add the flour mixture alternating with the milk to the butter mixture. Add the vanilla last. Spread evenly in the prepared pan. Bake for about 30 minutes or until done. Cut into oblong sticks to serve.

Banana Bars

Adapted from Favorite Recipes of the King's Daughters and Sons

MAKES 36 SERVINGS

½ cup unsalted butter, softened,
  plus more for greasing the pan
1 cup sugar
2 eggs
1 cup sour cream
2 ripe bananas, mashed
1 teaspoon vanilla extract
2 cups flour
1 teaspoon salt
1 teaspoon baking soda
powdered sugar and chopped
  walnuts, for sprinkling

Preheat the oven to 350°F. Grease the bottom and sides of a 15 x 10-inch jellyroll pan.

In a large bowl, cream the butter and sugar; add the eggs, then the sour cream, bananas, and vanilla. Mix well. Sift in the flour, salt, and baking powder, and mix. Pour the batter into the prepared jellyroll pan and bake for about 20 minutes. Cool and cut into bars, then dust with powdered sugar and nuts before serving.

Frosted Creams

MAKES 36 PIECES

⅓ cup unsalted butter, softened,
  plus more for greasing the pan
½ cup sugar
1 egg
½ cup molasses
1½ cups flour
½ teaspoon baking soda
2 teaspoons baking powder
½ teaspoon cinnamon
½ cup buttermilk
Frosting (see below)

Preheat the oven to 350°F. Grease the bottom and sides of a 13 x 9-inch baking pan.

In a large bowl, cream the butter with the sugar; add the egg. Mix in the molasses.

In a small bowl, sift together the flour, baking soda, baking powder, and cinnamon. Add the flour mixture alternating with the buttermilk to the butter mixture. Spread the batter in the prepared baking pan and bake until cooked through. Cool. Frost and cut into squares to serve.

Frosting

1 egg white
⅛ teaspoon cream of tartar
1 cup sugar

In a small bowl, beat the egg white with the cream of tartar until stiff.

In a small saucepan, boil the sugar with ⅓ cup water until it spins a thread (230°F to 234°F on a candy thermometer). Pour the sugar syrup slowly over the egg white and beat until smooth. Spread over the bars.

Frosted Honey Fruit Cookies

Contributed by B.N., Nebraska

MAKES 32 BARS

½ cup unsalted butter, softened, plus more for greasing the pans

1 cup brown sugar

1 egg

½ cup honey

2½ cups flour

1 teaspoon baking soda

½ teaspoon salt

1 teaspoon cinnamon

¼ teaspoon allspice

¼ teaspoon ground cloves

½ cup buttermilk

¼ cup raisins, dredged in a little flour

1 cup walnuts, chopped

¼ cup unsweetened shredded coconut

½ cup powdered sugar

¼ teaspoon vanilla extract

2 tablespoons milk (or less)

Preheat the oven to 375°F. Grease the bottom and sides of two 8-inch square baking pans.

In a large bowl, cream the butter and brown sugar; add the egg and honey.

In a small bowl, combine the flour, baking soda, salt, cinnamon, allspice, and cloves. Add the flour mixture alternating with the buttermilk to the butter mixture, then add the raisins, nuts, and coconut. Mix all together well, then spread the batter thinly into the two prepared baking pans. Bake for about 20 minutes.

As the bars are baking, prepare the icing: Combine the powdered sugar, vanilla, and just enough of the milk to make a thin, smooth paste.

Remove the bars from the oven. Spread a thin layer of icing over the bars while they are still warm. Allow them to cool, then cut the bars into squares or diamonds to serve.

Apricot Bars

MAKES 16 BARS

½ cup unsalted butter, softened, plus more for greasing the pan

¼ cup granulated sugar

1⅓ cups flour, divided

⅔ cup dried apricots

2 eggs

1 cup brown sugar

¼ teaspoon salt

½ teaspoon baking powder

½ cup walnuts, finely chopped

½ teaspoon vanilla extract

Preheat the oven to 350°F. Grease the bottom and sides of an 8-inch square baking pan.

In a medium-size bowl, combine the butter, granulated sugar, and 1 cup of the flour, then press the dough into the prepared baking pan. Bake for 15 minutes.

In a small saucepan, cook the apricots in 1 cup of water for 10 minutes, then drain, cool, and chop.

In a large bowl, beat the eggs, then add the apricots, brown sugar, salt, remaining ⅓ cup flour, baking powder, walnuts, and vanilla. Spread the mixture over the baked crust, then return the baking pan to the oven for an additional 30 minutes. Cool and cut into squares to serve.

Frosted Nut Cookies

MAKES 36 COOKIES

½ cup unsalted butter, softened,
    plus more for greasing the pan
1 cup granulated sugar
2 eggs, well beaten
1 teaspoon vanilla extract, divided
1½ cups flour
½ teaspoon salt
1 teaspoon baking powder
1 cup walnuts, chopped
1 egg white
1 cup brown sugar

Preheat the oven to 375°F. Grease the bottom and sides of a 15 x 10-inch jellyroll pan.

In a large bowl, cream the butter; add the granulated sugar and mix together well. Add the eggs and ½ teaspoon of the vanilla, and flour sifted with salt and baking powder. Spread ¼ inch thick on the prepared baking pan. Sprinkle with the chopped nuts.

In a small bowl, beat the egg white until stiff, then fold in the brown sugar and remaining ½ teaspoon vanilla. Spread the frosting over the cookie and bake for 20 minutes. Cut into squares before entirely cool.

Apple Oatmeal Torte

SERVES 16

½ cup unsalted butter, melted,
    plus more for greasing the pan
1 cup flour
½ teaspoon salt
½ teaspoon baking soda
1 teaspoon cinnamon
1½ cups rolled oats
½ cup brown sugar
1 egg
1 teaspoon vanilla extract
3 sour apples, cored, peeled, and
    sliced

Preheat the oven to 350°F. Grease the bottom and sides of a 9-inch square baking pan.

In a large bowl, sift together the flour, salt, baking soda, and cinnamon, then mix in the oats, sugar, butter, egg, and vanilla. Press half the mixture into the prepared baking pan and arrange the apple slices over it. Roll out the remaining dough and press it lightly over the apples. Bake for 25 to 30 minutes, until done. Cool and cut into bars to serve.

Lemon Bars

Adapted from The Meetinghouse Cookbook

No recipe arsenal is complete without light and tangy lemon bars. With only seven ingredients, these are baked in two stages: first, there's the sweet short crust, followed by the luscious lemon curd. Take them from the oven just as soon as the curd sets, otherwise they'll be rubbery. These bars are perfect for brunch, bake sales, and picnics.

MAKES 36 BARS

1 cup unsalted butter, softened,
   plus more for greasing the pan
2¼ cups flour, divided
½ cup powdered sugar, plus more
   for dusting
4 eggs
2 cups granulated sugar
⅓ cup lemon juice
½ teaspoon baking powder

Preheat the oven to 350°F. Grease the bottom and sides of a 13 x 9-inch baking pan.

In a large bowl, sift together 2 cups of the flour and the powdered sugar. Cut in the butter, then press the dough into the prepared baking pan. Bake for 20 to 25 minutes, until just done.

In a large bowl, beat together the eggs, granulated sugar, and lemon juice. Sift in the remaining ¼ cup flour and the baking powder and mix well. Pour the lemon mixture over the baked crust and return the baking pan to the oven for an additional 25 minutes, watching to make sure the curd doesn't overcook. Dust with powdered sugar and cool. Cut into bars to serve.

Filled Date Torte

SERVES 36

1 cup unsalted butter, melted, plus
    more for greasing the pan
40 dates, chopped
1 cup granulated sugar
½ teaspoon vanilla extract
1½ cups flour
½ teaspoon baking soda
½ teaspoon salt
1 cup brown sugar
1½ cups rolled oats
1 cup walnuts, chopped

Preheat the oven to 350°F. Grease the bottom and sides of a 13 x 9-inch baking pan.

In a small saucepan, combine the chopped dates with 1 cup of water and the granulated sugar. Cook the filling until it is thick and smooth, then stir in the vanilla. Set aside to cool.

Meanwhile, in a medium-size bowl, sift together the flour, baking soda, and salt, then mix in the brown sugar and oats. Add the melted butter and nuts and mix thoroughly with your hands. Pat half of the crumb mixture into the prepared baking pan. Spread the date mixture evenly into the baking pan, then add the remaining crumb mixture on top, patting it down well. Bake for 45 minutes. Cool and cut into strips or squares to serve.

Raspberry Meringue Bars

Adapted from The Meetinghouse Cookbook

MAKES 36 BARS

½ cup unsalted butter, softened
½ cup powdered sugar
2 eggs, separated
1 cup flour
1 cup raspberry jam
½ cup granulated sugar
1 cup almond flour

Preheat the oven to 350°F.

In a large bowl, cream the butter and powdered sugar, then add the egg yolks. Sift in the flour and mix. Press the dough into a 13 x 9-inch baking pan and bake for 10 to 15 minutes. Remove from the oven and allow to cool slightly.

Spread the baked cookie with the jam. In a small bowl, beat the egg whites until stiff, gradually adding the granulated sugar. Fold in the almond flour, then spread the meringue over the jam. Return the baking pan to the oven and bake for 25 more minutes, until golden. Cool and cut into squares to serve.

Cakes and Doughnuts

Phoebe Jane's Angel Food Cake

April 1937

You can serve it any time of year, but angel food cake is particularly suited for the warm spring and summer months as a refreshing dessert showcasing the fruits of the season. Start out with strawberries in the late spring, move on to cherries, then blueberries, and finally sweet, tree-ripened peaches at the peak of summer. If you're missing this light and easy cake in the heart of winter, simply top it with your favorite preserves or compote—and don't forget a dollop of cream!

SERVES 8 TO 12

1 cup sifted cake flour
1⅓ cups sugar, divided
1¼ cups egg whites
½ teaspoon salt
1 teaspoon cream of tartar
2 tablespoons water
1 teaspoon vanilla extract

Preheat the oven to 325°F.

In a small bowl, sift the flour once before measuring, then sift it again 4 times, together with ⅓ cup of the sugar.

In a large mixing bowl, beat the egg whites with a rotary beater. When the eggs are foamy, add the salt, cream of tartar, water, and vanilla. Beat just until the egg whites peak and are still moist and shiny. With a flat beater or mixing spoon, fold in the remaining 1 cup sugar, sifting 1 or 2 tablespoons at a time over the surface and gently folding it in (about 50 strokes). Fold in the sifted flour and sugar mixture in the same way (about 90 strokes). Pour the batter into an ungreased angel food cake pans and bake immediately for 1 hour or until the surface of the cake springs back into place when pressed lightly with your finger. It should be at its full height, have a delicate brown color, and be shrunken slightly from the sides of the pan. Let the cake cool in the inverted pan for an hour before removing.

Orange Sunshine Cake with Whipped Cream Topping

February 1936, contributed by L.H., Colorado

SERVES 8 TO 12

---

5 eggs, separated
1½ cups sugar, divided
½ cup orange juice
1½ cups cake flour
¼ teaspoon salt
½ teaspoon baking powder
¾ teaspoon cream of tartar
sweetened whipped cream, for
 topping
grated orange zest, for topping

Preheat the oven to 325°F.

In a large mixing bowl, beat the egg yolks until thick and light. Add ¾ cup of the sugar, followed by the orange juice, and beat.

In a small bowl, sift together the flour, salt, and baking powder 3 times, then add to the egg yolk mixture.

In a medium-size bowl, beat the egg whites until foamy, add the cream of tartar, then gradually add the remaining ¾ cup sugar. Fold the egg white mixture into the egg yolk mixture. Pour the batter into an ungreased tube pan and bake for 1 hour. Cool, remove the cake from the pan, and top with slightly sweetened whipped cream. Sprinkle with grated orange zest.

◆

Kiss Cake

June 1936

SERVES 4

---

butter for greasing the pan
3 large egg whites, at room
 temperature
pinch of salt
few drops lemon juice or vinegar
1 cup finely granulated sugar
1⅓ cups powdered sugar
whipped cream, for serving
strawberries, for serving

Preheat the oven to 250°F. Grease a baking sheet and cover it with parchment paper.

In a large mixing bowl, beat the egg whites until stiff and dry, gradually adding the salt as you work. Add the lemon juice or vinegar, then gradually add the granulated and powdered sugars, beating after each addition. When finished, the meringue will be very stiff and satiny in appearance.

On the prepared baking sheet, shape the meringue into 3 round, flat layers, making them graduated in size, with the largest one about 9 inches across. Bake for 45 minutes. The layers will be a very pale brown. Pile the whipped cream and strawberries between each layer, and spread whipped cream over the top.

Old-Fashioned Pound Cake

March 1938

SERVES 12 TO 16

1¾ cups butter, plus more for
    greasing the pan
1¾ cups sifted cake flour
1 teaspoon salt
¼ teaspoon baking powder
2 cups fine granulated sugar
8 eggs
2 tablespoons brandy
1 teaspoon mace or nutmeg

Preheat the oven to 300°F. Thoroughly grease a standard-size tube pan.

In a small bowl, sift together the flour, salt, and baking powder.

In a large mixing bowl, cream the butter very thoroughly and begin to add the sugar gradually. Cream the butter and sugar together until light and fluffy. Add 1 egg at a time and beat after the addition of each egg. Add the brandy and mace or nutmeg. Add the sifted dry ingredients and beat until light and fluffy. Transfer the batter to the prepared tube pan and bake for 1 hour, then turn off the heat but leave the cake in the oven for another 15 minutes. Pound cake is not usually iced. Store it in the pan in which it is baked.

White Cake with Cherry Frosting

February 1936

SERVES 12

½ cup butter (or part other fat),
    plus more for greasing the pans
1 cup sugar
3 egg whites, unbeaten
1 teaspoon vanilla extract
2 cups cake flour
1 tablespoon baking powder
¼ teaspoon salt
⅔ cup milk
Cherry Frosting (see page 203)

Preheat the oven to 375°F. Grease two 9-inch round cake pans.

In a large mixing bowl, cream the butter; add the sugar slowly, beating until fluffy. Add the unbeaten egg whites, one at a time, beating very thoroughly after each addition, then add the vanilla.

In a small bowl, sift together the cake flour, baking powder, and salt, then add the sifted dry ingredients to the butter mixture alternating with the milk. Pour the batter into the prepared cake pans and bake. Frost with cherry frosting.

Whipped Cream Cake with Boiled Marshmallow Icing

February 1939

SERVES 9 TO 16

butter for greasing the pans
1 cup heavy cream
2 eggs
1 cup sugar
1 teaspoon vanilla extract
1½ cups sifted cake flour
2 teaspoons baking powder
½ teaspoon salt
Boiled Marshmallow Icing
    (see page 203)

Preheat the oven to 350°F. Grease the bottom and sides of a 9-inch square baking pan or two 8-inch round cake pans, or insert paper liners in a cupcake pan.

In a large mixing bowl, whip the cream until it is stiff. Drop in the unbeaten eggs, one at a time, and the sugar, beating after each addition. (If the eggs are large, one white may be omitted.) Add the vanilla.

Sift together the flour, baking powder, and salt, and fold lightly into the mixture. Blend well. Bake for 25 to 30 minutes. Let the cake cool on a rack, unmold, and top with the icing.

Whipped Cream Cake with Caramel Icing: Replace the Boiled Marshmallow Icing with Caramel Icing (see page 204).

Raspberry Cake

December 1930, contributed by a reader from New York

SERVES 12

½ cup butter, plus more for
    greasing the pans
2 tablespoons buttermilk
1 teaspoon baking soda
1 cup sugar
2 eggs, beaten
2 cups flour
½ teaspoon cream of tartar
1 cup raspberries
Boiled Icing (see page 202)

Preheat the oven to 350°F. Grease the bottom and sides of two 9-inch cake pans.

In a small bowl, combine the buttermilk and the baking soda. Set aside.

In a large mixing bowl, cream the butter, add the sugar, and blend well. Add the eggs and the buttermilk mixture. Sift together the flour and the cream of tartar, then add them to the butter mixture, along with the raspberries. Pour the batter into the prepared cake pans and bake until done. When the cakes are cool, frost with the icing.

Coconut Cake with Seven-Minute Icing

February 1936, contributed by Mrs. J.M., New York

SERVES 12

⅓ cup butter (or part other fat),
    plus more for greasing the pans
1 cup sugar
1 whole egg
2 egg yolks, unbeaten
2 cups cake flour
2 teaspoons baking powder
¼ teaspoon salt
¾ cup milk
¼ teaspoon lemon extract or
    ½ teaspoon vanilla extract
Seven-Minute Icing (see page 203)
unsweetened grated coconut,
    for serving

Preheat the oven to 350°F. Grease the bottom and sides of two 9-inch round baking pans.

In a large mixing bowl, cream the butter thoroughly; add the sugar gradually and cream again. Add the egg and yolks and beat until creamy and light.

In a small bowl, sift together the flour, baking powder, and salt 3 times, then add the sifted dry ingredients to the butter mixture alternating with the milk. Add the lemon or vanilla extract and beat until smooth. Pour the batter into the prepared cake pans and bake until done. Let the cakes cool on a rack, unmold, and frost with the icing, sprinkling each layer thickly with unsweetened grated coconut.

German Apple Cake

May 1927, contributed by Mrs. E.I.K, North Dakota

SERVES 16

2 tablespoons butter or lard, plus
    more for greasing the pan and
    topping the cake
2½ cups flour
pinch of salt
1 teaspoon baking powder
1 cup milk
6 tart apples
sugar, for topping
cinnamon, for topping

Preheat the oven to 350°F. Grease the bottom and sides of a 9-inch square baking pan.

In a large mixing bowl, combine the butter, flour, salt, baking powder, and milk to make a dough. Turn the dough out onto a floured surface and roll out to ½ inch thick. Press the dough into the prepared baking pan, leaving a gap of 1 inch at the top.

Pare, core, and quarter the apples, then put them into the pan, standing the apples on end. Sprinkle with sugar, cinnamon, and bits of butter. Bake until cooked through and serve as any cake.

Basic Honey Cake

August 1933

SERVES 8

½ cup butter, plus more for greasing the pans

½ cup honey

½ cup sugar

2 eggs, beaten

2 cups cake flour

2 teaspoons baking soda

4 teaspoons baking powder

¼ teaspoon salt

⅓ cup milk

2 teaspoons cream

Preheat the oven to 350°F. Butter and line two 8-inch round baking pans.

In a large mixing bowl, cream the butter, honey, and sugar. Add the beaten eggs and beat until blended.

In a small bowl, sift together the cake flour, baking soda, baking powder, and salt, then add the sifted dry ingredients to the butter mixture alternating with the milk. Do not beat, just mix slightly to blend. Add the cream and pour the batter into the prepared cake pans. Bake for 20 minutes.

Harvest Layer Cake

October 1933

SERVES 12

½ cup butter, plus more for greasing the pans

3 cups sifted cake flour

1 tablespoon baking powder

½ teaspoon salt

1¼ cups brown sugar, firmly packed

3 egg yolks, unbeaten

1 cup milk

1½ teaspoons vanilla extract

frosting, for serving

chopped nuts (optional)

Preheat the oven to 375°F. Grease the bottom and sides of two 9-inch round baking pans.

In a medium-size bowl, sift the flour once, measure, add the baking powder and salt, and sift them together 3 times.

In a large mixing bowl, cream the butter thoroughly, add the brown sugar gradually, and cream together until light and fluffy. Add the egg yolks; beat well. Add the flour mixture alternating with the milk, a small amount at a time. Beat after each addition until smooth. Add the vanilla. Pour the batter into the prepared pans and bake for 30 minutes, or until done. Spread frosting between layers and on the top and sides of the cake. Sprinkle nuts over the top and sides of the cake while the frosting is still soft, if desired.

Lemon Layer Cake

February 1913

SERVES 12

---

butter and flour for greasing
    the pans
3 eggs
6 tablespoons sugar
grated zest of 1 lemon
6 tablespoons flour
1 teaspoon baking powder
1½ ounces butter, melted
Lemon Curd (see below)
powdered sugar, for serving

Preheat the oven to 350°F. Grease and flour the bottom and sides of two 8-inch round baking pans.

Put the eggs, sugar, and grated lemon zest into a double boiler and whisk until warm. Remove the mixture from the heat and continue whisking until quite cold and stiff.

Sift together the flour and baking powder, then add the flour mixture to the egg mixture, followed by the melted butter. Stir it very gently—do not beat the batter. Pour the batter into the prepared cake pans and bake for 10 minutes. Allow the pans to stand for 2 or 3 minutes before turning the cakes out.

When the cakes are cold, spread each thickly over with the lemon curd; place the rounds together, divide into 12 pieces, dust with powdered sugar, and serve.

Lemon Curd

¾ cup sugar
4 egg yolks
1 egg white
grated zest and juice of 1 large
    lemon, strained
4 tablespoons butter

In a saucepan, stir together the sugar, egg yolks, egg white, lemon zest and juice, and butter. Stir over a gentle heat until it thickens. Pour onto a plate, and cool before use.

Perfect Gingerbread

September 1930

The distinct taste of gingerbread is as special as the holiday season with which it is so closely associated. Fortunately, the warm welcome of cinnamon and ginger have the added benefit of soothing the stomach—something most of us could use during a month of overindulgent festivities. Enjoy with a hot cup of coffee or tea or a cold glass of milk.

SERVES 4

---

butter for greasing the pan
2 cups flour
½ cup sugar
1½ teaspoons ground ginger
½ teaspoon cinnamon
2 teaspoons baking powder
⅔ teaspoon baking soda
¼ teaspoon salt
¾ cup molasses
1 cup buttermilk
1 egg
4 tablespoons unsalted butter, melted
whipped cream, for serving

Preheat the oven to 350°F. Grease the bottom and sides of an 8-inch square baking pan.

In a medium-size bowl, sift together the flour, sugar, ginger, cinnamon, baking powder, baking soda, and salt.

In a large mixing bowl, combine the molasses, buttermilk, egg, and melted butter. Mix in the dry ingredients and beat until smooth. Pour into the prepared pan and bake for 20 to 30 minutes. Cut into squares and serve with a dollop of whipped cream.

Old English Gingerbread with Fruit Filling

Contributed by Mrs. H.E.CUP, Nebraska

SERVES 16

1 cup unsalted butter, softened, plus
    more for greasing the pans
1 cup molasses
1½ cups sugar, divided
1 cup buttermilk
2 eggs
1 tablespoon ground ginger
3½ cups flour
1 teaspoon cinnamon
1 teaspoon baking soda
1½ teaspoons nutmeg
1 teaspoon grated lemon zest
1 cup raisins
marshmallows (optional)
1 tablespoon lemon juice
¼ cup dried apricot pulp
1 tablespoon cornstarch
½ cup walnuts, chopped
½ cup dried figs, chopped
½ cup dates, chopped
Icing (optional)

Preheat the oven to 325°F. Grease the bottom and sides of two 8-inch square baking pans.

In a large mixing bowl, cream the butter; add the molasses and 1 cup of the sugar. Add the buttermilk, eggs, ginger, flour, cinnamon, baking soda, and nutmeg and mix well. Pour the batter into the prepared baking pans and bake for about 30 minutes, until firm.

Meanwhile, in a medium-size saucepan, stir the grated lemon zest into 1½ cups water, then add the raisins to soak. Marshmallows may be added, too, if using. Add the lemon juice, apricots, the remaining ½ cup sugar, cornstarch, walnuts, figs, and dates. Cook until thick.

When the cakes have cooled, spread the filling on one of the gingerbread layers, then put the other on top. Ice or not, as preferred. Cut into squares to serve.

Gingerbread Banana Shortcake

June 1928

SERVES 12

---

3 tablespoons shortening, plus more for greasing the pan

½ cup sugar

1 egg

½ cup molasses

1¾ cups flour

1 teaspoon ground ginger

½ teaspoon cinnamon

½ teaspoon salt

½ teaspoon baking soda

½ cup boiling water

sliced bananas, for serving

whipped cream, for serving

Preheat the oven to 350°F. Grease the bottom and sides of an 8-inch square baking pan.

In a large mixing bowl, cream the shortening and the sugar. Add the egg and the molasses.

In a small bowl, sift together the flour, ginger, cinnamon, salt, and baking soda, then add the sifted dry ingredients to the shortening mixture alternating with the boiling water. Pour into the prepared pan and bake for 25 to 30 minutes. While slightly warm, cover with sliced bananas and pile with whipped cream.

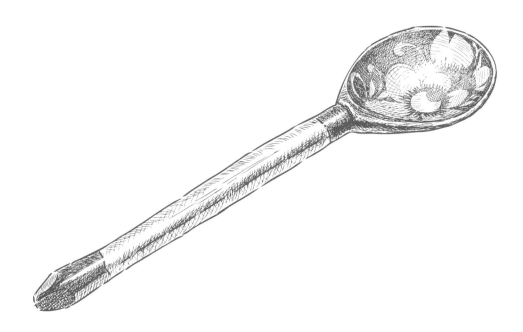

Old-Fashioned Strawberry Shortcake

1934

SERVES 8

¼ cup butter, plus more for greasing
    the pans and buttering the cakes
¾ cup milk
2 heaping cups flour, plus more for
    the pans
2 teaspoons baking powder
¼ teaspoon salt
2 teaspoons sugar, plus extra for
    the strawberries
plenty of strawberries
Chantilly Cream (see below)

Preheat the oven to 400°F. Butter and flour two 8-inch cake pans.

In a large mixing bowl, sift together the flour, baking powder, salt, and sugar. Rub in the butter with the tips of your fingers and add the milk gradually. Toss on a floured board, divide it in half, pat and roll out, transfer to the prepared cake pans, and bake for 15 minutes.

Sweeten the strawberries with sugar to taste and place the bowl on the back of the stove until the strawberries are warmed. Remove the cakes from the pans after baking and split and butter the insides. Crush the berries slightly and spoon a layer of berries between and on top of the cake layers. Cover the top with the cream and place one cake on top of the other.

Chantilly Cream

1 cup cream
¼ cup sugar
½ teaspoon vanilla extract

In a bowl, whip the cream, sugar, and vanilla together until soft peaks form.

Buttermilk Cupcakes

October 1914

MAKES 12 TO 16 CUPCAKES

1 cup buttermilk
1 teaspoon baking soda
pinch of salt
cloves
allspice
cinnamon
½ cup sugar
½ cup butter
1 egg, lightly beaten
1 cup molasses
2 cups sifted flour
Easy Fudge Icing (see page 204)

Preheat the oven to 350°F. Grease the cups of a 12-cup muffin pan or line them with paper liners.

In a small bowl, stir together the buttermilk, baking soda, salt, and cloves, allspice, and cinnamon to taste.

In a mixing bowl, beat the sugar, butter, and egg together. Pour the buttermilk mixture into the butter mixture, then add the molasses and the flour. Transfer the batter to the prepared muffin tins and bake until done. When the cupcakes are cool, frost with the icing.

Upside-Down Strawberry Crumb Cake

June 1936, contributed by Mrs. G.A.CUP, Louisiana

½ cup butter or part other fat
1 cup granulated sugar
3 eggs, beaten
2 cups dry sifted breadcrumbs
½ cup flour
1 teaspoon baking powder
⅛ teaspoon salt
1 cup milk
½ teaspoon almond extract
3 tablespoons butter, melted
¾ cup brown sugar
fresh strawberries
whipped cream, for serving

Preheat the oven to 350°F.

In a large mixing bowl, cream the butter or other fat and granulated sugar together thoroughly. Add the eggs.

In a small bowl, sift together the breadcrumbs, flour, baking powder, and salt, then add the sifted dry ingredients to the creamed mixture alternating with the milk and the almond extract.

Pour the melted butter into a 9-inch baking pan, then sprinkle the bottom with the brown sugar and whole or sliced strawberries, covering it thickly. Pour on the batter and bake for 40 minutes. When the cake is done, let it stand a few minutes, then turn it upside down onto a cake plate or platter. Serve with unsweetened whipped cream.

Blackberry Gingerbread Upside-Down Cake

September 1938

SERVES 8

2 cups flour
½ cup granulated sugar
1 teaspoon ground ginger
1 teaspoon cinnamon
½ teaspoon allspice
¼ teaspoon salt
½ teaspoon baking soda
1½ teaspoons baking powder
1 egg
¾ cup molasses
½ cup butter, melted
¾ cup hot water
4 tablespoons butter
¾ cup berry juice
¾ cup brown sugar
2 cups blackberries, washed and
    drained

Preheat the oven to 350°F.

In a small bowl, sift together the flour, granulated sugar, ginger, cinnamon, allspice, salt, baking soda, and baking powder.

In a large mixing bowl, combine the egg, molasses, melted butter, and hot water. Add the sifted dry ingredients and beat until well blended.

In a 9-inch cast-iron (oven-safe) skillet, bring the butter, berry juice, and brown sugar to a boil and boil for 2 minutes. Add the blackberries, spreading them around the bottom of the pan. Cover the blackberries and syrup with the batter, carefully spreading it so it covers all the fruit. Place the skillet in the oven and bake for 35 minutes. Let the cake stand in the pan for 15 minutes before turning it out, inverted, onto a plate or cake stand.

Pineapple Upside-Down Cake

September 1938

Even after the main part of your meal is cooking, it is not too late to start an upside-down cake. Stir it up, put it in the oven, and let it bake while the rest of the meal is being eaten. If you like a richer cake, sprinkle a few nuts in the syrup.

SERVES 8

1½ cups flour

1 cup granulated sugar

2 teaspoons baking powder

½ teaspoon salt

2 eggs, broken into a cup, which is then filled with rich milk or cream

1 teaspoon vanilla extract

1 (15-ounce) can pineapple, crushed or sliced, drained, ¾ cup juice reserved

4 tablespoons butter

¾ cup brown sugar

unsweetened whipped cream, for serving

Preheat the oven to 375°F.

Sift the flour, granulated sugar, baking powder, and salt together in a large mixing bowl. Add the egg mixture and vanilla and beat hard for 5 minutes. It is essential to beat the batter until it is smooth and fluffy for a light cake of fine texture. Set the batter aside.

Place the reserved pineapple juice, butter, and brown sugar in a deep 9- to 10-inch oven-safe skillet; bring the mixture to a boil and cook for 2 minutes, just long enough for the ingredients to blend together. Turn off the heat before the syrup becomes thick and candy-like. Place the pineapple in the juice mixture.

Cover the pineapple and syrup with the batter, spreading it so it covers all the fruit. Place the skillet in the oven and bake the cake for 30 minutes. Let the cake stand until it is partly cool, then turn it upside down onto a cake plate or platter to serve. Accompany it with unsweetened whipped cream.

Orange Upside-Down Cake: Follow the instructions above, but instead of a can of pineapple and its juice, use the juice of 1 large orange and 2 oranges sliced into thin rings. Put the juice, butter, and brown sugar in the skillet and bring it to a boil. Add the orange rings and boil for 2 minutes. Arrange the orange slices to cover the bottom of the skillet, overlapping if necessary, and pour on the cake batter. Bake for 35 to 40 minutes.

Spice Cake with Prune Topping: In the above cake recipe, omit the vanilla and add ½ teaspoon allspice, ½ teaspoon cinnamon, and ½ teaspoon ground cloves, sifting them in with the dry ingredients. For the topping, replace the pineapple and pineapple juice with ¾ cup prune juice and 2 cups well-drained unsweetened cooked and pitted prunes. Boil the juice, butter, and brown sugar in the skillet for 2 minutes. Cover the bottom of the skillet with the prunes, placing them skin-side down. Pour on the batter and bake for 30 minutes.

Lemon Roll

March 1936, contributed by Mrs. W.K., Minnesota

SERVES 8

---

butter for greasing the pan
6 eggs, separated
½ cup granulated sugar
1 tablespoon lemon juice
1 teaspoon grated lemon zest
½ cup cake flour
½ teaspoon baking powder
¼ teaspoon salt
powdered sugar
1 cup heavy cream, whipped
Lemon Sauce (see below)

Grease a 10 x 15-inch jellyroll pan and line it with parchment paper.

In a large mixing bowl, beat the egg whites, adding the granulated sugar gradually until stiff and smooth.

In a medium-size bowl, beat the egg yolks, add the lemon juice and zest, and then fold the yolk mixture into the egg whites.

Sift the flour, baking powder, and salt together 2 or 3 times, then fold the sifted dry ingredients into the egg mixture. Pour the batter into the prepared pan. Start in a cold oven, bringing the temperature up to 250°F. Bake just until firm but not brown.

Turn out onto a clean towel, sprinkled liberally with powdered sugar, and remove the parchment paper. Let the cake stand for about 30 minutes until cool, then roll the cake up in cloth like a jelly roll, rolling it the long way of the cake. Let stand for 10 minutes. Unroll, spread with part of the whipped cream, and roll up again. Sprinkle the roll with powdered sugar, wrap in waxed paper or parchment, and store in a cool place until serving. To serve, slice the roll into pieces. Top each piece with a spoonful of the remaining whipped cream and a spoonful of the sauce.

Lemon Sauce

---

1 cup sugar
grated zest and juice of 1 lemon
3 tablespoons cornstarch
⅔ cup water
1 egg or 2 yolks
½ tablespoon butter

Mix the sugar, lemon zest, cornstarch, and water in a double boiler and cook for 10 minutes, stirring until thickened. In a small bowl, beat the eggs, then slowly add a few tablespoons of the hot syrup, stirring constantly. Slowly add the egg mixture to the double boiler, stirring constantly. Stir in the butter, then add the lemon juice. Cool.

Sour Cream Crullers

August 1916

MAKES ABOUT 2 DOZEN CRULLERS

---

cooking oil
1 teaspoon baking soda
½ cup sour cream
½ cup butter
1½ cups granulated sugar
1 small egg
2½ cups flour, plus more if needed
powdered sugar
a little grated nutmeg

In a deep fryer or large, deep saucepan, heat 3 to 4 inches of oil to 375°F.

In a small bowl, combine the baking soda and sour cream.

In a large mixing bowl, cream the butter and granulated sugar, add the egg, then the soda sour cream mixture and the flour. Mix well, adding more flour if necessary so as to make a dough that will roll out easily (it should be as soft as can be handled). Turn the dough out onto a lightly floured surface. Roll out the dough to a ¼-inch thickness, shape with a cutter, and fry to a golden brown. Drain on thick brown paper for a moment, then roll in powdered sugar while still warm. Sprinkle nutmeg on top.

Note: These crullers, when properly made, are not as liable to absorb the grease as a recipe in which more shortening is used.

Grandmother's Crullers

MAKES 2 TO 3 DOZEN CRULLERS

---

6 cups lard or cooking oil
2 cups granulated sugar
4 eggs, or less if they are scarce
1 cup buttermilk
½ teaspoon baking soda
4 to 6 cups flour
powdered sugar (optional)

In a stockpot or a deep saucepan, heat the lard or oil to 375°F.

In a large mixing bowl, combine the granulated sugar, eggs, buttermilk, baking soda, and enough of the flour to make a smooth paste. Turn the dough out onto a lightly floured surface and roll out thin. Cut the dough into 3-inch squares. Beginning ½ inch from one end, cut the squares into 3 or 4 strips. Braid these, or twist them into fancy shapes, and fry them in the hot lard. Drain the crullers on paper and sprinkle with powdered sugar, if desired.

Pumpkin Doughnuts

Doughnuts can be a fun treat to experiment with at home. The key is to get the oil to 375°F; with the first addition of dough, the temperature will drop. Keep it to a steady 360°F thereafter. Too hot, and the doughnuts will burn; too cold, and they'll be greasy and soggy. Cook them until the doughnuts float, turn them with a slotted spoon, and cook for 45 seconds; turn and cook for 45 seconds longer before removing.

MAKES 2 TO 3 DOZEN DOUGHNUTS

---

6 cups lard or cooking oil
3 eggs, lightly beaten
1 cup sugar
1 cup sour cream
1 scant teaspoon baking soda
pinch of salt
2 teaspoons cinnamon
1 teaspoon nutmeg
1 cup pumpkin purée
4 to 6 cups flour
cinnamon sugar, for rolling

In a deep fryer or large, deep saucepan, heat 3 to 4 inches of oil to 375°F.

In a large mixing bowl, combine the eggs, sugar, sour cream, baking soda, salt, cinnamon, nutmeg, pumpkin purée, and just enough flour to make a soft but rollable dough. Turn the dough out onto a lightly floured surface. Roll out the dough to a ½-inch thickness, shape with a cutter, and fry to a golden brown. Drain on thick brown paper for a moment, then roll in cinnamon and sugar while still warm.

Molasses Doughnuts

MAKES 2 TO 3 DOZEN DOUGHNUTS

cooking oil
2 eggs
1 cup molasses
2 tablespoons shortening, melted
1¼ teaspoons baking soda
½ teaspoon salt
¼ teaspoon nutmeg
¼ teaspoon ginger
½ teaspoon cinnamon
5 to 6 cups flour, sifted, divided
1 cup buttermilk

In a deep fryer or large, deep saucepan, heat 3 to 4 inches of oil to 375°F.

In a large mixing bowl, beat the eggs, then stir in the molasses and shortening.

In a small bowl, sift together the baking soda, salt, nutmeg, ginger, cinnamon, and 2 cups of the flour, then add the sifted dry ingredients to the egg mixture alternating with the buttermilk. Add more sifted flour to make a stiff dough. Turn the dough out onto a lightly floured surface. Roll out the dough to a ⅜-inch thickness and cut the dough into strips. Twist the strips, fold them in half, twist them again, and pinch the ends together. Fry the doughnuts in the hot oil. Drain on brown paper.

Fried Cakes

June 1910

MAKES ABOUT 3 DOZEN CAKES

6 cups lard or oil
1 teaspoon baking soda
2 cups buttermilk
2 cups sugar
2 eggs
1 teaspoon salt
3 tablespoons lard, melted
1 teaspoon grated nutmeg
5 to 6 cups flour

In a stockpot or a deep saucepan, heat the lard or oil to 375°F.

In a small bowl, combine the baking soda and buttermilk.

In a large mixing bowl, combine the sugar, eggs, salt, melted lard, and nutmeg. Stir until the mixture is like cream, then pour in the buttermilk mixture. Add just enough of the flour to make a stiff dough. Turn the dough out onto a lightly floured surface. Roll out the dough as soft as possible, shape with a doughnut cutter, and fry to a golden brown.

Snowballs

Contributed by Mrs. Tschida

MAKES ABOUT 2 DOZEN SNOWBALLS

---

cooking oil
2 egg yolks
1 tablespoon heavy cream
a few drops of vanilla extract
pinch of salt
1 teaspoon cider vinegar
1 teaspoon powdered sugar, plus
    extra for dusting
1 to 2 cups flour

In a deep fryer or a large, deep saucepan, heat 3 to 4 inches of oil to 375°F.

In a large bowl, blend the egg yolks, cream, vanilla, salt, vinegar, powdered sugar, and enough flour to stiffen the dough. Turn the dough out onto a lightly floured surface, then roll it out thin and cut it into 1-inch circles. Drop the rounds in the hot oil to cover, and with a fork, lift up points as the ring fries to make it like a rosette. Fry to a very light brown, drain, and sprinkle with powdered sugar before serving.

Corn Fritters

November 1912

MAKES ABOUT A DOZEN FRITTERS

---

cooking oil
1 cup corn, cut off the cob
2 cups flour
pinch of salt
1 tablespoon sugar
1½ tablespoons baking powder
maple syrup, for serving

In a deep fryer or a large, deep saucepan, heat 2 to 3 inches of oil.

In a large bowl, mix together the corn, flour, salt, sugar, baking powder, and enough water to make a thick batter. Drop the batter by spoonfuls into the hot oil. Cook until nicely browned on all sides. Drain on paper towels. Serve with maple syrup.

Banana Fritters

Contributed by L.S., Nevada

SERVES 8

---

4 large, firm bananas
powdered sugar
lemon juice
cooking oil
1 cup flour
½ teaspoon salt
2 eggs
⅔ cup milk

Peel the bananas. Cut each banana in half lengthwise, then in half again crosswise. Sprinkle each piece of banana with powdered sugar and a little lemon juice and let them stand for an hour.

In a deep fryer or a large, deep saucepan, heat 3 to 4 inches of oil.

In a large bowl, mix the flour, salt, eggs, and milk, beating well. Dip each piece of banana in the batter and fry in the hot oil. Drain on brown paper.

Funnel Cakes

Adapted from The Pennsylvania Dutch Cook Book

You can thank German immigrants, called the Pennsylvania Dutch (a mistranslation of the word Deutsch), for this favorite carnival treat. It's called a "funnel" cake because the loose batter is dropped into the hot oil through a funnel, which helps in making the loopy, lacy shapes. To get the authentic experience, drench the hot cakes in powdered sugar.

MAKES 12 TO 24 FUNNEL CAKES

---

cooking oil
4 cups milk
4 eggs, beaten
½ teaspoon baking soda dissolved
    in 1 teaspoon water
2 tablespoons sugar
pinch of salt
4 cups flour

In a deep fryer or a large, deep saucepan, heat 3 to 4 inches of oil.

In a large mixing bowl, combine the milk, eggs, baking soda mixture, sugar, salt, and just enough flour to make a batter that will run smoothly through a funnel. Pour the batter through a funnel into the hot oil; twist and turn the funnel to make shapes. Drain on brown paper.

Apple Fritters

SERVES 8

cooking oil
2 eggs, separated
½ cup honey
1 cup sour cream
2 cups flour
½ teaspoon nutmeg
½ teaspoon salt
½ teaspoon baking soda
1 tablespoon unsalted butter, melted
4 sour apples, peeled, cored, and
    sliced into ¼-inch rings

In a deep fryer or a large, deep saucepan, heat 3 to 4 inches of oil.

In a large bowl, beat the egg yolks and honey until smooth, then mix in the sour cream. Sift in the flour, nutmeg, salt, and baking soda, then stir in the butter.

In another bowl, beat the egg whites until they are stiff, then fold the egg whites into the batter.

Dip the apple rings in the batter and fry them in the hot oil, turning once to brown on both sides. Drain on brown paper.

Boiled Icing

December 1925

MAKES ENOUGH FOR A 2-LAYER 9-INCH CAKE OR 24 CUPCAKES

¾ cup water
1¾ cups sugar, divided
3 egg whites
tiny pinch of salt (optional)
1 teaspoon extract of your choice
1 level teaspoon baking powder

In a saucepan, bring the water to a boil. Reserve 1½ tablespoons of the sugar, then dissolve the remaining sugar in the boiling water. Cover the saucepan to prevent the sugar from adhering to the sides of the pan and boil rapidly for a few minutes. When heavy drops fall from a spoon when the spoon is held high above the saucepan, beat the egg whites* and salt (if using) in a separate bowl. When the egg whites are well beaten, add the reserved sugar and beat well until the egg whites are stiff but not dry. Test the boiling syrup again. If it silks to a long thread that flies out, it is ready to be poured very slowly over the egg whites as you continue beating vigorously. Stir in the extract. After beating about 5 minutes, add the baking powder. Continue beating until the icing cools and is smooth and glossy.

Note: Wait until the syrup begins to thicken before beating the egg whites because if beaten egg whites stand, they will liquefy. If desired, a tiny pinch of salt may be added to the whites before beginning to beat.

Boiled Marshmallow Icing

February 1939

MAKES ENOUGH FOR A 2-LAYER 9-INCH CAKE OR 24 CUPCAKES

2½ cups sugar
½ cup light corn syrup
¼ teaspoon salt
2 egg whites
1 teaspoon vanilla extract
8 large marshmallows, cut into
    quarters

Cook the sugar, corn syrup, salt, and ½ cup water together in a saucepan to the firm ball stage (250°F registered on a candy thermometer).

Beat the egg whites until they form peaks, then slowly pour the hot syrup into the egg whites, beating constantly. Add the vanilla and continue beating until the frosting will hold its shape when tossed over the back of a spoon. Stir in the marshmallows.

Seven-Minute Icing

February 1939

MAKES ENOUGH FOR A 1-LAYER 9-INCH CAKE (DOUBLE IT FOR 2 LAYERS)

---

1 cup sugar
1 egg white
1 tablespoon syrup or honey
few grains of salt
½ teaspoon vanilla extract

Combine the sugar, egg white, syrup or honey, salt, and ¼ cup water in a double boiler. Cook over boiling water for 7 to 10 minutes, beating all the while with a rotary beater. When the icing is thick and almost ready to spread, remove it from the stove. Add the vanilla and beat until cool and ready to spread. Double the recipe for all but a small cake.

Cherry Frosting

February 1936, contributed by A.A.F., Wisconsin

MAKES ENOUGH FOR A 1-LAYER 9-INCH CAKE OR 12 TO 16 CUPCAKES

---

1 cup sugar
⅛ teaspoon cream of tartar
1 egg white, beaten
few drops almond extract
⅓ cup chopped maraschino or
    preserved cherries, drained*

In a small saucepan over medium heat, combine the sugar and the cream of tartar with ½ cup water, stirring until the sugar is dissolved. Then cook without stirring until the syrup spins a good thread (candy thermometer reading of 240°F).

Beat the egg white until it forms peaks, then slowly pour the hot syrup over the egg white, beating constantly. Add the almond extract and the cherries, and continue to beat until thick and ready to spread.

Note: The cherries must be well drained of juice or the frosting will be too soft.

Easy Fudge Icing

February 1936

MAKES ENOUGH FOR A 1-LAYER 9-INCH CAKE (DOUBLE IT FOR 2 LAYERS)

---

2 tablespoons butter, softened
1 whole egg or 2 egg yolks
a few grains of salt
1 (1-ounce) square unsweetened
    chocolate, melted
½ teaspoon vanilla extract
2 cups powdered sugar
cream, as needed

In a mixing bowl, combine the butter, egg, salt, and chocolate and beat with a rotary beater until creamy. Add the vanilla, the powdered sugar, and enough cream to make the icing easily spreadable.

Caramel Icing

February 1936

MAKES ENOUGH FOR A 2-LAYER 9-INCH CAKE

---

2 cups sugar
1 cup thin sweet or sour cream
3 tablespoons Caramel Syrup
    (see below)
1 tablespoon butter
1 teaspoon grated orange zest

Boil the sugar, cream, and syrup until the mixture forms a soft ball in cold water (candy thermometer reading of 234°F to 240°F). Remove the pan from the heat and let the mixture cool somewhat. Add the butter and the grated orange zest and beat until thick and creamy.

Caramel Syrup

---

2 cups sugar
1 cup hot water

In a smooth, heavy skillet, melt the sugar until golden brown. Avoid overheating, or the syrup will have a burned taste. Add the hot water, stir until the caramel is dissolved, and boil until it forms a heavy syrup. Cool, then store in a jar until needed. Makes about 2 cups.

Pies and Tarts

Plain Pastry for Pie Crust

1934

MAKES A 9-INCH SINGLE CRUST

½ teaspoon salt
1½ cups sifted flour
½ cup lard or shortening
3 or 4 tablespoons ice cold water

Add the salt to the flour and cut in the lard or shortening with a dough blender, sharp-tined fork, or your fingertips, until the pieces are the size of small peas. Add a little water at a time, mixing with a fork lightly until it can be shaped into a ball. Roll out the dough, handling it as little as possible. Work quickly, especially in warm weather, so the fat doesn't melt. To bake a single crust, lay the crust in the pie tin quite loosely and prick well over the bottom or fit over the bottom of an inverted tin. Bake at 450°F.

Note: Tough crust may be due to too much water and too little fat, overhandling, or too cool an oven. A soggy under crust may be due to not having the oven hot enough to bake the under crust before the filling soaks in, or to having the crust so rich or rolled so thin that the filling breaks through.

Meringue Topping

MAKES ENOUGH TO TOP A 9-INCH PIE

2 egg whites
2 tablespoons sugar
¼ teaspoon vanilla extract

Beat the whites until they are stiff but not dry. Add the sugar and beat until smooth and glossy. Add the vanilla, spread on top of pie, and bake.

Chess Pie

April 1931, contributed by Mrs. D., Tennessee

SERVES 8

8 egg yolks
3 cups sugar
¼ cup cream
1 teaspoon vanilla or lemon extract
unbaked pie pastry (see above)

Preheat the oven to 300°F.

In a large bowl, mix together the egg yolks, sugar, cream, and vanilla or lemon extract. Pour the filling into the pie crust and bake for 30 minutes.

Angel Pie

April 1939

SERVES 8

---

6 tablespoons butter, softened
1 cup flour
¾ cup plus 3 tablespoons sugar
3 tablespoons cornstarch
1 cup hot water
grated zest and juice of 1 lemon
3 egg whites
¼ teaspoon salt
⅓ cup whipping cream
⅓ cup crushed peanut brittle

Preheat the oven to 400°F.

In a medium-size bowl, blend together the butter, flour, and 3 tablespoons of the sugar. Put into an 8-inch pie pan and bake for 15 minutes. Cool.

For the filling, in a medium-size saucepan, combine the remaining ¾ cup sugar and the cornstarch. Add the hot water and cook for 10 minutes, stirring until thick. Add the grated lemon zest, cool slightly, and add the lemon juice.

Beat the egg whites with the salt until the egg whites are stiff, then fold them into the lemon mixture. Pour the filling into the pre-baked shell and let stand until firm.

Whip the cream, then spread it on the top of the pie. Sprinkle with the crushed peanut brittle. (Or a color scheme may be carried out with the use of other crushed candy.)

Buttermilk Pie

September 1934, contributed by Mrs. S.G.P., Wisconsin

SERVES 8

---

unbaked pie pastry (see Plain
   Pastry for Pie Crust, page 206)
2 tablespoons butter
2 tablespoons flour
2 egg yolks, beaten
1 whole egg, beaten
1½ cups sugar
1 tablespoon lemon juice
2½ cups buttermilk

Preheat the oven to 450°F. Fill a 9-inch pie plate with the pie crust (or other single crust pie pastry).

In a large bowl, cream the butter and flour together. Add the beaten yolks and the whole egg. Add the sugar, lemon juice, and buttermilk, stirring well. Pour the filling into the pastry-lined pie plate and bake for 10 minutes. Lower the temperature to 350°F and bake until the filling is quivery and just barely set at the center (it should not be soupy), about 40 minutes.

Cream Pie

1934

SERVES 8

2 cups rich milk, divided
½ cup sugar
¼ cup cornstarch or ⅓ cup flour
¼ teaspoon salt
2 egg yolks, beaten
1 teaspoon vanilla extract
baked 9-inch pie shell (see Plain Pastry for Pie Crust, page 206)
Meringue Topping (see page 206)

Preheat the oven to 425°F.

Scald 1¾ cups of the milk in a double boiler. In a small bowl, mix the remaining ¼ cup milk with the sugar, cornstarch, and salt and add to the hot milk. Cook for 10 minutes, stirring constantly. Stir a few spoonfuls of the hot custard into the egg yolks, then slowly stir the egg yolk mixture into the double boiler. Cook for 3 to 5 minutes, then add the vanilla and cool slightly. Pour the custard into the baked pie shell. Cover the custard with the meringue and bake for 20 minutes.

Banana Cream Pie: Arrange sliced bananas in the baked shell, pour on the custard, and finish as directed above.

Strawberry Cream Pie: Arrange sliced strawberries in the baked shell, pour on the custard, and finish as directed above.

Pineapple Cream Pie: Spread canned pineapple in the baked shell, pour on the custard, and finish as directed above.

Rhubarb Pie

April 1925

SERVES 8

3 cups diced and scalded rhubarb
1 cup sugar
⅛ teaspoon salt
1 teaspoon cinnamon
1 tablespoon butter
baked 8- or 9-inch pie shell (see Plain Pastry for Pie Crust, page 206)

Preheat the oven to 300°F.

In a large bowl, mix the rhubarb, sugar, and salt; sprinkle with the cinnamon and dot with the butter. Place in an uncovered baking dish and cook slowly until the rhubarb is tender and some of the juice has evaporated.

Transfer the cooked rhubarb to the pie shell and serve hot.

Variation: Add ½ cup raisins to 2 cups of rhubarb and proceed as directed above.

Michigan Cherry Pie

Contributed by Annabelle Jones, Michigan

SERVES 8

3 cups cherries, canned without sugar, drained, with juice reserved

1 cup cherry juice

1¼ cups sugar

2 batches unbaked Plain Pastry for Pie Crusts (see page 206) or other double crust pie pastry

3½ tablespoons cornstarch

2 tablespoons butter

½ teaspoon almond extract

In a large bowl, mix the cherries, cherry juice, and sugar. Allow to stand for 5 minutes.

Meanwhile, mix up the pastry for the crust. Transfer the dough to the refrigerator to cool.

Drain the juice from the cherries, transferring the juice to a saucepan. Mix the cornstarch with a little of the juice until smooth. Bring the remaining juice to a boil, then stir in the cornstarch mixture. Boil, stirring constantly, for 1 minute. Remove the saucepan from the heat and stir in the butter. Set aside to cool.

Meanwhile, preheat the oven to 425°F. Roll out the dough for the pie crust and put one of the crusts into an 8- or 9-inch pie plate.

Add the cherries and the almond extract to the cooled, thickened juice; pour the filling into the pastry shell. Cover the pie with the top crust; press down on the edges with the tines of a fork. Cut off excess pastry and pierce the dough to vent. Bake until the crust is golden brown, about 45 minutes.

Cherry-Blueberry Pie: Substitute 1 cup blueberries for 1 cup cherries.

Cherry-Raspberry Pie: Substitute 1 cup raspberries for 1 cup cherries.

Ohio Cherry Pie

Contributed by Eleanor Enos, Ohio

SERVES 8

2 batches unbaked Plain Pastry for Pie Crust (see page 206) or other double crust pie pastry

1 cup sugar, divided, plus more for dusting

pinch of salt

2 tablespoons flour

3 cups drained, unsweetened canned cherries

¼ cup juice

milk

Preheat the oven to 425°F. Line an 8- or 9-inch plate with the pastry. Sprinkle the bottom crust with a little flour.

In a medium-size bowl, mix together ½ cup of the sugar, salt, and flour.

Spread half (1½ cups) of the cherries over the bottom of the pie, then sprinkle them with the sugar mixture. Add another layer of the remaining cherries and juice, and sprinkle with the rest of the sugar mixture. Place the top crust on the pie, and make cuts to allow for steam to escape. Brush the top with milk, then sprinkle lightly with the remaining ½ cup of sugar. Bake for 10 minutes, then reduce the heat to 350°F and bake for 30 to 40 minutes longer, until the crust is nicely golden and the filling is set.

Lattice-Top Strawberry-Cherry Pie

June 1936

This is the star-crossed lovers of pie. When made with fresh fruit, it could only be done when both strawberry and sour cherry seasons overlap, in late June or early July in many parts of the country. Luckily, this recipe uses canned cherries, which also provide deliciously tart juice. Don't stress the lattice top: roll your top crust into more of a rectangle than a circle, chill it, then cut 8 strips, about 1 inch wide, with a pastry wheel or pizza cutter. Let them warm up a bit before assembling. (And don't worry about weaving them—the crisscross pattern alone will wow everyone!)

SERVES 8

1½ cups sour red cherries, drained, with ¼ cup of juice reserved*

2½ tablespoons fine tapioca

1 cup sugar

pinch of salt

2 batches unbaked Plain Pastry for Pie Crust (see page 206) or other double crust pie pastry

1 cup fresh strawberries, sliced

1 teaspoon butter

Preheat the oven to 450°F.

In a large bowl, combine the reserved cherry juice, tapioca, sugar, and salt and let it stand as you line an 8- or 9-inch pie plate with one batch of the pastry and cut the second batch of pastry into strips for the lattice top.

Add the cherries and the strawberries to the juice mixture and pour it into the pie shell. Dot with the butter and top with the pastry strips. Seal the edges of the pie, building up a rim or binding with parchment pie tape, a special bit of equipment readily available from kitchen supply stores that helps prevent juice overflow and reduces edge darkening. Bake for 10 minutes, then reduce the oven temperature to 350°F and bake for another 25 minutes.

*Note: Fresh or canned cherries, pitted and unsweetened, may be used.

Pear Coronet Pie

April 1938

SERVES 8

½ cup flour
⅔ cup sugar
⅛ teaspoon salt
2 cups milk, scalded
2 teaspoons butter
3 egg yolks
¾ teaspoon vanilla extract
2 to 3 drops almond extract
baked 9-inch pie shell (see Plain
    Pastry for Pie Crust, page 206)
6 to 8 canned pear halves, well
    drained
cherries, preserved ginger, or
    red jelly
Meringue Topping (see page 206)

Preheat the oven to 325°F.

In a double boiler, combine the flour, sugar, and salt. Add the scalded milk slowly, stirring well. Cook over hot water, stirring often, until the mixture is thick and smooth. Add the butter. Beat the egg yolks slightly, then add a few spoonfuls of the hot mixture to the yolks. Stir the yolks quickly into the filling, continuing to stir until the eggs thicken. Remove the filling from the heat and cool before adding the vanilla and almond extracts.

Fill the cooled, baked pastry shell with the filling. Arrange the pears, rounded end toward the rim of the pastry and hollow-side up, pressing lightly so that the surface of the pears is flush with the filling. Fill the hollows of the pears with whole or chopped cherries, chopped preserved ginger, or a bit of red jelly. Fill the space between the pears and in the center of the pie with the meringue. Bake until the meringue is brown.

Raspberry Pie

May 1910

SERVES 6 TO 8

1 pint raspberries
3 tablespoons granulated sugar
2 tablespoons water
butter the size of an egg
1 tablespoon powdered sugar
1 tablespoon fine breadcrumbs
almond extract
2 egg yolks, well beaten
2 egg whites, whipped stiff
unbaked pie pastry (see Plain
    Pastry for Pie Crust, page 206)

Preheat the oven to 400°F.

Put a pint of berries in a granite saucepan, add the granulated sugar and water, and shake over the heat just until the juice flows freely (do not let the berries lose their shape). Skim out the berries and transfer them to a bowl, then boil the syrup until clear.

In a mixing bowl, cream together the butter and powdered sugar. Add the breadcrumbs, a few drops of almond extract, and the beaten egg yolks. Fold in the stiff egg whites.

Line an 8-inch pie plate with the unbaked pastry. Spread the raspberries across the pastry, pour the syrup over them, and spread the berries with the egg mixture. Bake until baked through.

Cranberry Molasses Pie

November 1929

SERVES 8

2 batches unbaked Plain Pastry for
    Pie Crusts (see page 206) or
    other double crust pie pastry
1 quart (4 cups) ripe cranberries
1 tablespoon butter
1 cup brown sugar
1 cup granulated sugar
1 cup molasses

Preheat the oven to 300°F. Roll out the pastry; line a deep 9-inch pie plate with one batch of pastry, and cut the other batch into strips.

In a large saucepan, combine the cranberries, butter, brown sugar, granulated sugar, and molasses. Cook over low heat for 10 minutes, then pour into the pastry-lined pie plate. Cover with strips of crust, arranged crisscross. Bake for 45 minutes to 1 hour, or until the berries are thoroughly cooked.

Individual Pumpkin Pies

November 1921

MAKES 6 MINI PIES

⅔ cup brown sugar
½ cup steamed and strained pumpkin
2½ cups milk
2 eggs
1 teaspoon cinnamon
½ teaspoon ground ginger
½ teaspoon salt
1 teaspoon grated lemon zest
6 individual unbaked pie shells*
whipped cream, for serving

Preheat the oven to 300°F.

In a large bowl, mix together the brown sugar, pumpkin, milk, eggs, cinnamon, ginger, salt, and lemon zest. Pour the filling into the pie shells and bake until done. Cool the pies before serving them with whipped cream.

*Note: Individual unbaked pie shells, between 4½ and 5 inches in diameter, can be found at bakers' supply shops.

Sweet Potato Pie

February 1910

Though sweet potato pie might not be the national fall-time treasure that pumpkin pie is, it does deserve a place at the table. Though similar in texture, the best sweet potato pies aren't just masked versions of pumpkin pie. This recipe calls for steaming the sweet potato, but a baked sweet potato concentrates the flavor (without adding extra moisture). Take care to remove the pie from the oven just as soon as it is barely set in the center.

SERVES 8

---

unbaked pie pastry (see Plain
    Pastry for Pie Crust, page 206)
3 eggs, separated
2 cups milk
½ cup sugar
2 medium sweet potatoes, peeled
    and steamed (about 1 cup)
cinnamon
1 tablespoon butter, melted
Meringue Topping (see page 206)

Preheat the oven to 350°F. Line a 9-inch pie plate with the pastry.

In a large bowl, beat the egg yolks until they are light, then add the milk and sugar.

Press the sweet potatoes through a sieve, then stir the pulp into the milk and egg mixture. Season with the cinnamon and butter. Transfer the filling to the prepared pie plate. Bake until done. After baking the pie, make the meringue using the egg whites, spread the meringue over the top of the pie, and return the pie to the oven to brown.

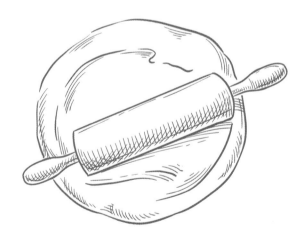

Colonial Innkeepers Pecan Pie

March 1938

SERVES 8

---

unbaked pie pastry (see Plain
    Pastry for Pie Crust, page 206)
3 eggs
½ cup sugar
¼ teaspoon salt
1 teaspoon vanilla extract
1 cup dark corn syrup
1 cup butter, melted
1 cup whole pecan meats

Preheat the oven to 350°F. Line a 9-inch pie plate with the pastry.

In a large bowl, beat the eggs; add the sugar, salt, and vanilla and beat lightly. Add the syrup and butter. Place the pecans in the bottom of the pastry-lined pie plate, and pour in the filling. Bake in for 50 to 60 minutes.

Lemon Tart

February 1937

SERVES 12 TO 16

For the Filling:
6 tablespoons flour
2 cups sugar
2 cups milk
grated zest and juice of 2 lemons
2 eggs, lightly beaten

For the Crust:
3½ cups sifted flour
½ teaspoon baking soda
½ teaspoon salt
1 cup sugar
¼ cup butter
¼ cup lard
⅔ to ¾ cup buttermilk

Preheat the oven to 400°F.

To make the filling, mix the flour, sugar, and milk together and cook in a saucepan over moderate heat until thick and smooth, about 5 minutes. Add the lemon zest and juice and gradually whisk in the eggs. Cool slightly.

To make the crust, sift together the flour, baking soda, salt, and sugar. Work in the butter and lard with a dough blender, sharp-tined fork, or your fingertips, until the pieces are the size of small peas. Add the milk a little at a time, mixing it lightly with a fork to make a soft dough. Roll out the dough, making 2 rounds and extra for top strips.

Fit the rounds into two small pie tins. Put half of the filling in each tin and lay the strips, 3 inches wide, across the top. Bake for 10 minutes, then lower the temperature to 350°F and continue baking until the crust is brown and the filling is puffed and just set.

Apple Tart

February 1937

SERVES 8

3½ cups plus 3 tablespoons sifted flour, divided

½ teaspoon baking soda

¼ teaspoon salt

1½ cups plus 2 tablespoons sugar, divided

4 tablespoons butter, plus more for topping the apples

¼ cup lard

⅔ to ¾ cup buttermilk

cinnamon

3 to 4 apples

¼ cup boiling water

ice cream or whipped cream, for serving

Preheat the oven to 375°F.

In a large bowl, sift together 3½ cups of the flour, the baking soda, salt, and 1 cup of the sugar. Work in the butter and lard with a dough blender, sharp-tined fork, or your fingertips, until the pieces are the size of small peas. Add the buttermilk a little at a time, mixing lightly with a fork to make a soft dough. Roll out the dough, and place it in a 10-inch tart pan.

In a small bowl, combine the remaining 3 tablespoons of flour with 2 tablespoons of the sugar. In another small bowl, combine the remaining ½ cup sugar with cinnamon, to taste.

Peel and core the apples. Cut the apples in half lengthwise, from stem to blossom end. In the bottom of the pastry-lined tin, sprinkle the sugar and flour mixture. Put in the apples, round side up. Sprinkle the sugar and the cinnamon over the top of the apples, then dot with butter. Pour in 3 tablespoons of water. Bake until the apples are soft, about 40 minutes.

As soon you remove the tart from the oven, pour in about ¼ cup boiling water, shaking until it is absorbed. Serve the tart slightly warm, plain or with ice cream or whipped cream as a special treat.

Applesauce Cheese Tarts

October 1935

MAKES 4 OR 5 MINI TARTS

---

1 cup flour

¼ teaspoon salt

⅓ cup butter

¼ cup grated Cheddar cheese, plus more for garnish

2½ to 3 tablespoons ice water

2 to 3 cups applesauce (see Old-Fashioned Applesauce, page 118)

whipped cream, for garnish

Sift the flour and salt together in a mixing bowl; cut in the butter with a pastry blender or two knives until the particles are the size of wheat grains. Stir in the grated cheese. Add the ice water by teaspoonfuls, tossing with a fork until all the flour is moistened. Gather the dough into a ball and divide it into 4 or 5 portions, one for each mini tart. Shape the dough into balls, flatten them on a floured board, and roll out each ball to fit over the bottoms of inverted tart or muffin tins. Trim the dough to fit and prick all over with a fork. Chill for 30 minutes.

Preheat the oven to 425°F. When the oven is ready, bake for 10 to 15 minutes, until the crust is slightly browned. Remove the crusts from the pans and cool. When cold, heap the chilled applesauce into the shells and garnish with grated cheese or stiffly whipped cream.

Cream Puffs

March 1931

Cream puffs are a county fair favorite, so it might surprise you to learn they involve two very French pastry techniques: pâte à choux *(for the puffs) and* crème pâtissière *(for the filling). But don't let that intimidate you. Once you make these, you'll discover how easy and fun they are. You can also skip the puff and pipe them 3 inches long for éclairs, drizzling them with melted chocolate after they're filled.*

MAKES ABOUT 2 DOZEN 3-INCH PUFFS

½ cup butter, plus more for
    greasing the pan
1 cup flour
4 eggs
Cream Filling (see below) or
    whipped cream

Preheat the oven to 350°F. Grease the bottom of a baking sheet.

Heat 1 cup of water and the butter in a saucepan until the water boils, then add the flour all at once and stir vigorously. Cook until the mass is thick and smooth. When it is thick enough it will ball up on the spoon. Remove the saucepan from the heat and add the eggs, unbeaten, one at a time, stirring after each addition. Beat until the dough is smooth. Drop the batter by spoonfuls onto the prepared baking sheet. Bake for 25 to 30 minutes, until the tops are golden brown. When the puffs are cool, make an incision in the side and fill with the cream filling or whipped cream.

Cream Filling

---

2 cups milk
¾ cup sugar
½ cup flour
⅛ teaspoon salt
2 eggs
1 teaspoon vanilla extract

Heat the milk in a double boiler. Mix the sugar, flour, and salt together, then whisk them into the hot milk. Bring the mixture to a boil.

In a small mixing bowl, slightly beat the eggs, then add a few spoonfuls of the hot milk mixture, whisking constantly. Slowly pour the egg mixture into the double boiler, whisking constantly. Reduce the heat and cook for a few minutes until the cream thickens. Remove from the heat, cool, and stir in the vanilla. *(Makes about 2½ cups.)*

Chocolate Cream Filling: Add 1 square unsweetened chocolate to the double boiler before boiling the milk.

Whipped Cream Filling: A filling of flavored and sweetened whipped cream may be used in the cream puffs if desired (see Chantilly Cream on page 190).

Cherry Turnovers

June 1910

1 cup butter, plus more for greasing
    the pan
1 pound flour
1 cup ice water
sweetened canned or freshly
    stewed stone cherries
2 eggs, well beaten
lemon juice
powdered sugar, for serving

Preheat the oven to 375°F. Grease a baking sheet.

Rub the butter into the flour using a pastry blender or your fingertips. When the particles are like coarse meal, moisten with just enough of the ice water to form a paste, handling the dough as little as possible. Roll out on a floured board, fold up, then roll out a second and then a third time. If the dough is still very cold, use it at once; if not, set it in the refrigerator until it is chilled.

Roll out the cold dough and cut it into 3-inch rounds, the size of large biscuits.

Drain the juice off the cherries and chop them. Mix the chopped cherries with the eggs and a little lemon juice. Put 1 tablespoon of the cherry mixture on one-half of each round of the crust, fold the other half to cover the cherries, and pinch the edges together to make half circles. Lay these half-circles on the prepared baking sheet, cut vent slits in the top, and bake to a golden brown. Sift sugar over them and serve either hot or cold.

Apple Roly-Poly

February 1925

3½ tablespoons butter, divided,
    plus more for greasing the pan
    and brushing the pastry
¾ cup plus 1 tablespoon granulated
    sugar, divided
½ teaspoon cinnamon
2 cups plus 1½ tablespoons
    bread flour, divided
5 teaspoons baking powder
½ teaspoon salt
2 tablespoons lard
⅔ to ¾ cup milk
4 sour apples, pared, cored, and
    chopped*
½ cup light brown or maple sugar
grated zest and juice of ¾ lemon

Preheat the oven to 350°F. Grease the bottom and sides of a 2-inch deep 13 x 9-inch glass baking pan.

In a small bowl, combine 1 tablespoon of the granulated sugar and the cinnamon. Set aside.

In a large mixing bowl, sift together 2 cups of the bread flour, baking powder, and salt. Work in 2 tablespoons of the butter and the lard with a fork or a pastry blender. Add just enough of the milk to make a soft dough. Turn the dough out onto a floured board and pat it into a 1-inch thick oblong. Brush with some butter and sprinkle with the cinnamon sugar. Over this, sprinkle the chopped apples. Roll the dough like a jelly roll and cut into 8 slices. Place the slices cut-side up in the prepared baking dish, leaving a little space between the slices.

In a small saucepan, boil 1½ cups of water. Stir in the brown sugar, remaining 1½ tablespoons of butter, lemon zest and juice, remaining ¾ cup of granulated sugar, and remaining 1½ tablespoons of flour. Boil for 6 minutes. Pour half of the sauce over the apple and pastry slices. Bake for 40 minutes. Serve drizzled with the remaining sauce.

*Note: Dried apples, soaked and chopped, may be used.

Peach Dumplings

September 1912

MAKES 4 TO 6 DUMPLINGS

---

2 cups flour
1 tablespoon baking powder
1 teaspoon salt
4 tablespoons fat
⅔ cup milk
4 to 6 small peaches, peeled, pitted, and sliced
sugar
butter
1 cup boiling water
cream, for serving

Preheat the oven to 350°F.

Sift together the flour, baking powder, and salt; quickly work in the fat with a fork or dough blender. Add the milk all at once and stir lightly to make a soft dough. Turn the dough out onto a lightly floured board and knead lightly for a few seconds. Roll the dough thin and cut into 5½-inch circles (saucer-size). Place a peeled and sliced peach in the center of each round, sprinkle the peaches with sugar and small pieces of butter, then pull up the edges of the dough and pinch it together securely at the top. Place the dumplings in a deep pan with pieces of butter, sugar, and peach slices surrounding them. Pour the boiling water over the peaches and place the pan in the oven at once. Bake for 30 minutes, until nicely browned. Serve hot, with sugar and cream.

Rhubarb Dumplings

April 1923

MAKES 6 DUMPLINGS

---

2 cups flour
4 tablespoons baking powder
½ teaspoon salt
2 tablespoons lard or butter
¾ cup milk
2 cups diced and scalded rhubarb
1½ cups sugar, divided
2 cups water

Preheat the oven to 400°F.

In a mixing bowl, sift together the flour, baking powder, and salt. Cut in the lard or butter with a dough blender, sharp-tined fork, or your fingertips, until the pieces are the size of small peas. Add the milk a little at a time, mixing lightly with a fork to make a soft dough. Divide the dough into 6 equal parts and roll each into a ½-inch-thick circle.

Mix the rhubarb with a ½ cup of the sugar and spoon the mixture equally in the center of each of the 6 dough circles. Bring the edges of the dough around the rhubarb, pinching it in place.

In an oven-proof skillet or baking dish, combine the water and the remaining 1 cup of sugar. Bring the mixture to a boil. Lay the dumplings smooth-side up in the boiling syrup. Place the dumplings in the oven and bake for 35 to 40 minutes.

Southern Apple Dumplings

October 1938

---

1 cup chopped, peeled apple

2 teaspoons lemon juice (not if apples are tart)

2 cups plus 2 tablespoons flour, divided

2 teaspoons baking powder

1 teaspoon salt, divided

½ cup plus 2 tablespoons butter, divided

¾ cup milk

2 cups granulated sugar

½ cup brown sugar

dash of nutmeg, if desired

vanilla ice cream, for serving

Preheat the oven to 425°F.

In a bowl, combine the apple and the lemon juice. Set aside.

In a mixing bowl, sift the flour, measure 2 cups, and then resift it with the baking powder and ½ teaspoon of the salt. Work in 2 tablespoons of the butter with your fingertips; when well blended, add the milk and stir vigorously until the dry ingredients are wet. Turn the dough out onto a floured board, knead very slightly to make the dough smooth, and roll out to ¼-inch thickness. Cut into 6 to 8 squares. In the center of each square, place 2 to 3 tablespoons of the chopped apples. Wet the edges of the dough and pinch it together around the apples.

In a deep, oven-safe skillet or baking pan (about 10 inches in diameter), combine the granulated sugar, brown sugar, nutmeg, and remaining 2 tablespoons of flour, and remaining ½ teaspoon of salt. Add 2 cups of water and the remaining ½ cup of butter, and cook with constant stirring until a thick sauce forms.

Drop the dumplings, seam-side down, into the boiling hot sauce. Cover the skillet or baking pan, place it in the oven, and bake for 30 minutes. Then remove the cover, baste the dumplings with the sauce, and continue cooking uncovered until the dumplings are golden brown. Serve the dumplings with the sauce and a scoop of vanilla ice cream.

Fruit Roll

February 1933, contributed by A.B.M., Indiana

SERVES 8

---

1 pint canned peaches
½ teaspoon ground cinnamon
½ cup brown sugar
1 teaspoon lemon juice
2 cups flour
1 tablespoon baking powder
1 teaspoon salt
4 tablespoons fat
⅔ cup milk
whipped cream, for serving

Preheat the oven to 425°F. Grease a 10 x 15-inch jellyroll pan and line it with parchment paper.

In a medium-size bowl, combine the peaches with the cinnamon, brown sugar, and lemon juice.

In a large mixing bowl, sift together the flour, baking powder, and salt. Quickly work in the fat with a fork or a dough blender. Add the milk all at once and stir lightly to make a soft dough. Turn the dough out onto a slightly floured board and knead lightly for a few seconds. Roll the dough into a ½-inch-thick rectangle or oblong shape and spread the dough with the seasoned peaches. Roll up the dough as for a jelly roll. Transfer the roll to the prepared pan. Bake for about 40 minutes, until done. Cut into individual servings. Serve with whipped cream.

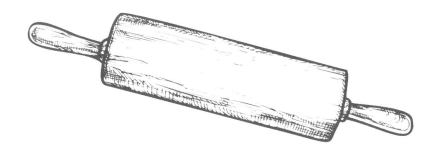

Herby Pasty

September 1932, contributed by Boscastle

MAKES ABOUT 8 PASTIES

1 pound flour
½ teaspoon salt
½ pound lard and suet (or butter
    or shortening)
ice water
chopped parsley
shallots, minced
spinach
boiling water
bacon, cooked and chopped
egg, well beaten

Preheat the oven to 450°F.

In a large bowl, combine the flour and salt, then rub the fat into the flour using a pastry blender or your fingertips. When the particles are like coarse meal, moisten with just enough ice water to form a paste, handling the dough as little as possible. Roll out about ¼ inch thick and cut into rounds of your desired size. Lay the rounds on the pastry board with half the round over the rolling pin.

Wash and chop equal quantities of parsley and shallots, and a half quantity of spinach. Pour boiling water over the parsley and spinach and let sit for ½ hour, then squeeze out all the moisture. Spoon the spinach mixture onto one-half of each pastry round, along with the shallots and bacon. Dampen the edges lightly and fold the dough over to cover the filling, forming a semi circle. Shape the pasty nicely and pinch up the edges of the pasty, except at one point. Pour the egg in at the opening, then finish pinching the edge to seal. Cut a slit in the center of the pasty, lay it on a baking sheet, and bake.

Chicken Pasty: Fill the pasty with cooked, boneless chicken cut up in small pieces.

Note: The Cornish pasty is the staple dish of the country. When the pasties are being made, each member has his or hers marked at one corner with the initial of the prospective owner. The true Cornish way to eat a pasty is to hold it in the hand and begin to bite it from the opposite end to the initial so that should any of it be uneaten, it may be consumed later by the rightful owner.

Beverages

Hot Cocoa

1934

SERVES 4 TO 6

---

2 tablespoons cocoa
2 tablespoons sugar
a few grains salt
1 cup boiling water
3 cups scalded milk
vanilla extract

Mix the cocoa, sugar, and salt in a saucepan; add boiling water gradually. Boil for 5 minutes. Add the milk and a few drops of vanilla; cook for 5 minutes longer or until smooth.

Fruit Lemonade

August 1919

SERVES 4

---

2 lemons
1 orange
¾ cup sugar
4 slices pineapple
ice

Squeeze the juice from the lemons and half the orange into a bowl. Add the sugar and stir well, then add 4 cups of water and stir until the sugar is all dissolved. Slice the remaining half of the orange into ¼-inch slices, cut the pineapple slices into quarters, and add to the bowl. Set the bowl into a cold place until ready to serve.

Plain Lemonade: Omit the orange and pineapples.

Rhubarb Punch

July 1932, contributed by S.D.A.CUP

SERVES 6
---

3 cups chopped rhubarb
1½ cups sugar
1 cup orange juice
3 tablespoons lemon juice
2 cups ice water

In a saucepan, cook rhubarb in 3 cups of water until the rhubarb is very soft. Rub the rhubarb through a fine strainer. Add the sugar to the strained juice and stir until it dissolves. Chill.

Add the orange juice, lemon juice, and ice water, and pour into glasses to serve.

Switchel

August 1923

SERVES 1
---

1 teaspoon sugar
1/16 teaspoon powered ginger
2 teaspoons boiled cider

This is a favorite summer drink for the eastern haymaker and harvester. Put the sugar, powdered ginger, and boiled cider in a glass and fill with water. Stir.

Variations: Vinegar and molasses may be substituted for the boiled cider, half and half.

Punch

August 1923

---

4 oranges

2 lemons

1 cup sugar

Squeeze the juice from the oranges and lemons.

Boil the sugar and ½ cup water until the syrup reaches the thread stage (223°F to 235°F on a candy thermometer). Add the orange and lemon juice and stir. This is the foundation punch.

Combine the juice mixture with enough water to make 2 quarts of punch.

For a minty undertone: 1 cup chopped mint leaves may be steeped in boiling water and strained out, and the resulting minty water can be substituted for part of the water in the punch.

Berry Punch: Use equal parts foundation punch and berry syrup.

Cherry or Currant Punch: Use 3 parts foundation to 1 part cherry or currant juice.

Ginger Punch: Boil ½ pound cut ginger in the foundation punch.

Grape Punch: Use equal parts foundation punch and grape juice.

Lemonade

August 1912

SERVES 4

3 whole lemons
¼ cup sugar
lemon slices, for serving

Wash the lemons well before using, scrubbing them lightly with a small brush; rinse and dry. Roll the lemons until they are soft and grate off the yellow zest, being careful not to get any of the bitter white pith. Cut the lemons in two and squeeze out the juice. Combine the lemon juice with the lemon zest, sugar, and 1 quart of water. Let stand for half an hour before serving. Add a freshly cut slice of lemon to each glass.

Note: The water may be poured boiling hot over the lemon and sugar and then cooled, if you wish.

Raspberryade

July–August 1921

SERVES 2

1 cup raspberry juice
2 teaspoons lemon juice
1 teaspoon sugar
3 bruised mint leaves

Stir together the raspberry juice, lemon juice, sugar, mint leaves, and 1 cup of water until the sugar is dissolved. Place on ice to cool before serving.

Resources

Alley, Lynn. *The Gourmet Slow Cooker, Volumes I and II.* Berkeley, CA: Ten Speed Press, 2003, 2006.

American Cooking: New England. New York: Time-Life Books, 1970.

Berolzheimer, Ruth, ed. *United States Regional Cook Book.* Garden City, NY: Garden City Publishing, Inc., 1939.

Cohasset Entertains. Cohasset, MA: The Garden Club of Cohasset, 1979.

Cooking Favorites of Vergennes. Vergennes, VT: Students Going to Europe, date unknown.

Davidson, Alan. *The Penguin Companion to Food.* New York: Penguin Books, 2002.

Favorite Recipes of the King's Daughters and Sons. Chautauqua, NY: International Order of the King's Daughter's and Sons, 1978.

Hensperger, Beth, and Julie Kaufman. *Not Your Mother's Slow Cooker Cookbook.* Boston: The Harvard Common Press, 2005.

Hot Recipes. Georgia, VT: Georgia Firewoman's Auxiliary, date unknown.

Hutchinson, Ruth. *The Pennsylvania Dutch Cook Book.* New York: Harper & Brothers, 1948.

The Meetinghouse Cookbook. Concord, MA: Women's Parish Association, 1974.

Our Favorite Recipes. Metuchen, NJ: Women's Guild of the Presbyterian Church, date unknown.

Out of Vermont Kitchens. Burlington, VT: Women of St. Paul's Cathedral, 1999.

Recipes from Maa Eway. Mahwah, NJ: Evening Department Women's Club of Mahwah Cook Book Committee, 1958.

Recipes Tried and True by Cooks. Windsor County, VT: Members of the Home Demonstration Clubs of Windsor County, 1941.

Soper, Musia, ed. *Encyclopedia of European Cooking.* London: Spring Books, 1962.

Index